The Sporting Life

Susan Davis and Sally Stephens
with the Exploratorium

An Exploratorium Book

An Owl Book
Henry Holt and Company   New York

Henry Holt and Company, Inc.
Publishers since 1866
115 West 18th Street
New York, New York 10011

Henry Holt® is a registered trademark
of Henry Holt and Company, Inc.

Published in Canada by Fitzhenry & Whiteside Ltd.,
195 Allstate Parkway, Markham, Ontario L3R 4T8

Library of Congress Cataloging-in-Publication Data
Stephens, Sally.
 The sporting life / Sally Stephens, Susan Davis, and
the Exploratorium.—1st American ed.
  p. cm.
 "An Owl book."
 Includes bibliographical references and index.
 ISBN 0-8050-4540-6 (pbk. : alk. paper)
 1. Physics. 2. Sports. 3. Force and energy.
I. Davis, Susan, 1950– . II. Exploratorium (Organization)
III. Title.
QC28.S74 1997   97-11914
530—dc21

Henry Holt Books are available for special promotions
and premiums. For details contact: Director, Special Markets.

First American edition 1997

Designed by Gary Crounse

Be careful! The experiments in this publication were designed
with safety and success in mind. But even the simplest activity
or most common materials can be harmful when mishandled
or misused.

Printed in the United States of America
All first editions are printed on acid-free paper. ∞

10 9 8 7 6 5 4 3 2 1

Contents

Introduction

Welcome to the Accidental Scientist, a series of books created by the Exploratorium to help you discover the science that's part of things you do every day.

In *The Sporting Life*, we investigate the science of muscles and sweat, of running shoes and golf balls, of whirling skaters and colliding football players. We answer the questions that come up when people are watching or playing sports. Does your grip on a baseball bat affect how far you hit the ball? Why do long jumpers keep running in the air? Why do you sometimes feel sore the day after you lift weights?

Along with the answers are experiments that you can use to find answers of your own. Measure your reaction time with an ordinary ruler. Toss a book in the air to get a better feel for the spins of an Olympic diver. Try some cool tricks with Superballs.

At the Exploratorium, San Francisco's museum of science, art, and human perception, we believe that learning how things work is not only fascinating and fun—but can also expand and enrich your experience of your favorite activities. Knowing how exercise affects your heart can help you improve your workout. Learning how your foot absorbs the shock of each footstep can help you choose sports shoes that better protect your feet. Understanding the science behind a curveball may help you know when a pitcher is throwing one—or maybe it will just make you feel better if you miss it.

Be warned: we've found that once you start noticing the science in sports, you may find it difficult to stop. You'll find yourself noticing things that you never paid any attention to before and asking questions that you never thought to ask. Have fun!

Goéry Delacôte
Director
Exploratorium

1 With a Body Like Yours

PRIOR TO THE 1996 Olympics, Annie Leibovitz took a striking photo of a group of Olympic hopefuls. In the center of the image, two athletes present a startling contrast: gymnast Dominique Moceanu perches on the shoulder of weight lifter Mark Henry. Dominique Moceanu weighs 72 pounds; Mark Henry weighs almost six times as much—415 pounds. At 25 inches around, Henry's arms are thicker than Moceanu's tiny waist.

Both are noted for their outstanding athletic abilities and achievements. But Henry probably wouldn't cope well with the rigors of the balance beam; Moceanu wouldn't excel in a competition involving heavy lifting.

Obviously, different bodies are good for different sports. Tall people are good at batting things out of the sky, like basketballs and volleyballs. Short people are good at doing things in small spaces—like double somersaults, followed by backflips, followed by cartwheels. Strong people are good at lifting things (like barbells) and throwing things (like discuses and other people). Lighter people are good at things that, well, require lightness. Runners aren't heavy because it's too hard to move their own mass; jockeys need to be light to ease the load on the horse.

But overall size is just one small part of what makes a person well-suited to a sport. Body proportions matter too. So do age, gender, and metabolism. And no matter what kind of body someone starts with, training can result in amazing changes. Through training, an athlete can change his or her body's shape, its strength—even the structure and function of its cells.

It Ain't the Size, It's the...

Size is important—you wouldn't see a 335-pound tackle like William ("the Refrigerator") Perry crouched on a thoroughbred. Nor would you see a tiny jockey, like William Klinke (just 4'3" and 103 pounds), tackling a quarterback. But size isn't everything. In 1996, the strongest man in the world (pound for pound) was Turkey's Naim Suleymanoglu, nicknamed "Pocket Hercules." Suleymanoglu is just 4'11" tall and weighs just 141 pounds. But at the 1996 Olympics, he lifted 413.5 pounds in the clean and jerk and 325 pounds in the snatch.

A physical attribute that's as important as size is proportion. One reason Pocket Hercules can lift so much is because "he has the ideal weight lifter's body," says Anthony Bartkowski, director of communications for the U.S. Weight Lifting Association. "He has short legs, short arms, and a short torso, so he can get under the bar easily." A long-legged person would have to squat farther down to get the bar; a long-armed person would have to thrust the weight farther in the air. If that champion weight lifter decided to join a crew team, his proportions would work against him. Rowers need long arms and long torsos, because the length of the sweep of the oars affects the speed with which they row. Similarly, discus throwers need long arms because that allows them to whip the discus with more speed. Tennis players benefit from long arms because they can create monster serves.

Each sport has its own requirements. Shot-putters need smaller, more compact bodies so they can spin in a smaller circle. Athletes who leap, like basketball players and long jumpers, often have long Achilles tendons (as do kangaroos). And those who need to cover distance often have long legs.

Now, you can't change something like your height (although wearing Air Jordans can give you a good 2.5 inches more). And you can't really change things like your limb-to-torso proportion. But you can change one aspect of your size: your weight. Wrestlers and boxers often fast or sit in saunas to drop weight before a match; female gymnasts, figure skaters, and swimmers, as well as both male and female jockeys, struggle with weight so much they often develop long-term eating disorders. (Jockeys who throw up their food to keep their weight down are called "flippers"—many admit to doing this.) And one 1996 Harvard study found that 62 percent of elite female gymnasts have eating disorders even after they retire. Lack of food causes some athletes to lose so much strength, concentration, and reaction time it affects their performance. Gymnast Christy Henrich became so weak from anorexia she was once pulled from an international meet. She died from the effects of anorexia in 1994.

Steve Hyche, an Arizona Cardinals linebacker, ate five steaks daily one season to gain 26 pounds. When asked about his experience, he said, "I never got full. But I got tired of chewing."

Sometimes athletes have to work to *gain* weight, rather than to lose it. In 1985, Michael Spinks became the first light-heavyweight (less than 175 pounds) to win a heavyweight title (more than 195 pounds), when he gained enough to turn himself into a 200-pounder. Linemen in football are currently getting bigger and bigger, so big, in fact, that a 300-pounder is practically small fry. And since 1988, Konishiki, the 6'1" Samoan sumo wrestler who won the Emperor's Cup, Japan's most prestigious sumo championship, has bounced up and down—from 488 pounds to 553 pounds to 504 pounds to 626 pounds. He has basically yo-yo dieted, gaining and loosing a chunk of blubber the size of Pocket Hercules.

Muscles: What You've Got and What You Can Get

You can also change the composition of your size by fiddling around with your muscles. The human body contains 639 muscles, which make up about 40 percent of the body's weight. Each muscle has anywhere from a few hundred to hundreds of thousands of muscle cells, also called "fibers," each of which can be several inches long. When you flex a muscle (which is a bunch of muscle fibers bound together), two proteins in each fiber, called *actin* and *myosin,* combine and form a protein complex, which shortens the fibers and contracts the muscles. For the muscles to do this work, they need energy, which comes primarily from a molecule called ATP or *adenosine triphosphate.*

Physiologists divide muscle fibers into two main types. Fast-twitch muscle fibers contract and relax very quickly. That makes them good for explosive and fast movements, like running a sprint, or hoisting a 400-pound barbell up in the air. Slow-twitch muscle fibers take up to ten times as long to contract and release. That makes them better suited for endurance events, like running a marathon or swimming across the English Channel.

Both fast-twitch and slow-twitch muscles use ATP to supply the energy they need to contract. But the two types of fiber make the ATP that they need in two different ways. Slow-twitch muscles get the energy they need to make ATP by breaking down fat and carbohydrate molecules carried by the blood. That's a process that requires oxygen, which is carried by hemoglobin in red blood cells. When you exercise aerobically, you are working at a pace that allows your heart and lungs to supply your muscles with enough oxygen to convert fuel molecules in your blood to the energy that the muscles need to contract.

Your fast-twitch muscles rely on a different system to produce most of their ATP. Rather than waiting for your heart and lungs to supply fuel and oxygen, fast-twitch muscles draw on stores of *glycogen* (which is formed from glucose) and break it down without oxygen—anaerobically—to make ATP. One of the by-products of this synthesis is the lactic acid that makes your muscles burn when you exercise anaerobically.

Of course, your muscles' stores of glycogen will only last so long—generally, they're good for about ten minutes of intense activity. Once those stores are used up, the muscles get exhausted and you can't go on until you've rested and gotten more oxygen into your system.

Most muscles are composed of both fast-twitch and slow-twitch fiber types, although some muscle groups have more of one than the other. You can see this most clearly in a chicken. The dark meat on the legs and thighs is slow-twitch fiber; the light meat on the breasts and wings is fast-twitch fiber. In humans, the back and neck muscles are classic slow-twitch muscles, while the eyelids, quadriceps, and biceps are predominantly fast-twitch.

Whether you're a sprinter or a marathon runner may depend in large part on what type of muscle fiber you have. Some elite athletes have a skewed distribution of fast- and slow-twitch muscle. Track and field star Carl Lewis has about 85 percent fast-twitch; marathoner Alberto Salazar has 92 percent slow-twitch. There is considerable debate about whether or not, by training, you can convert your slow-twitch muscles to fast-twitch, or vice versa. The general consensus is that you cannot. But you can develop each type of muscle and thereby enhance each set's performance through exercise.

Fast and Slow Twitch

Most of your muscles are a mix of fast- and slow-twitch fibers, with percentages of each varying from person to person and even from muscle to muscle. Other mammals are more specialized.

These photos show actual cross-sections through muscle fibers from two different animals. Each oval shape is a separate muscle fiber, and fast-twitch fibers have been stained to appear dark. The animal on the left has almost entirely fast-twitch muscles; the one on the right, almost entirely slow-twitch. Can you guess what animals they come from and which one is faster? If you guessed a fleet-footed cheetah (left) and a narwhal, a slow-moving marine mammal, you'd be right.

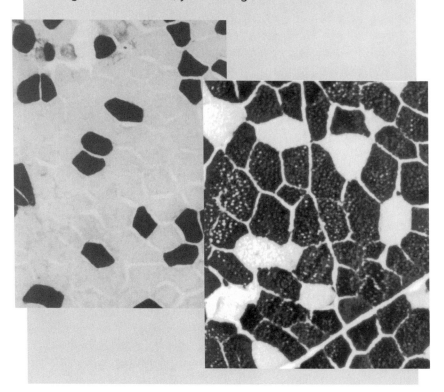

Clothespin Party Trick

• Take an ordinary clothespin (the spring-loaded kind) and hold it between your thumb and index finger. Get a watch with a second hand.

• Now see how many times you can open and close the clothespin in one minute.

• When your minute is up, DON'T STOP. See how many times you can open and close it during a second full minute.

What's going on?

Odds are you slowed down significantly during your second minute. What are you, some kind of weakling who can't twitch your fingers for two minutes without getting tired? Nope, it's just a question of how your muscles get the energy they need to function.

When you were opening and closing the clothespin, your muscles were exercising anaerobically, drawing on their stores of glycogen to produce the ATP molecules that supply the energy they need to contract. As the glycogen ran out, your muscles ran low on ATP and their ability to contract decreased.

If you were to squeeze the clothespin slowly, you would be exercising aerobically. In aerobic exercise, your muscles also draw on oxygen and the glucose and fatty acids carried in by the blood to produce ATP. Your ability to keep exercising aerobically depends on the delivery of oxygen and fuel molecules (glucose and fatty acids) to your muscles. And that depends on your circulation and respiration. (See pages 13–14.)

When you work out, you don't actually increase the number of muscle fibers—that's set at birth. But high-intensity, short-term exercise, like weight lifting, develops the thickness of the fibers, which increases the strength of their contractions. Different kinds of weight lifting develop different kinds of muscles. Body builders tend to work on one muscle at a time, to create definition (called "hypertrophy" by the scientists and "bulging" by the rest of us). Weight lifters are more concerned with strength than bulge, so they exercise whole groups of muscles. That's why when you see a weight lifter in a professional competition, he doesn't look as muscular as a body builder. In fact, he may look downright chubby. But he can lift considerably more.

Low-intensity, long-duration exercise (like long-distance running) actually decreases the muscle fiber's diameter and strength. But it provides a big endurance boost.

Scientists often study muscle development by studying other species. Some put rats on treadmills for several hours a day to simulate marathon running. Others give rats "high-resistance" tasks to simulate weight lifting. Still others, like Steve Doberstein, a molecular biologist at the University of California, Berkeley, study much tinier athletes. Doberstein uses an electron microscope to study muscular development in the embryos of fruit flies, which are about the size of a grain of sand. Embryonic fruit flies develop their muscles really fast, within a few hours. And once the muscles are developed, "they're really dramatic," Doberstein says. "There are mitochondria everywhere."

What are mitochondria, and why are they so exciting? The mitochondria are little factories in each cell that aerobically produce the energy the cell needs. They use oxygen (which is carried by hemoglobin in red blood cells) and convert fat and carbohydrates into ATP—at a rate of about 10 million molecules per second! Slow-twitch muscles tend to have numerous mitochondria, since they rely on mitochondria to produce the energy they need to contract. Fast-twitch muscles have fewer mitochondria.

By training, you are increasing the mitochondria in your muscles. "Through processes no one understands in the slightest," Doberstein says, "both slow and fast fiber types develop larger

Jogging won't help your weight-lifting ability—although it will certainly improve your cardiovascular condition. When your heart is good at delivering blood and oxygen, your endurance improves.

amounts of mitochondria. You can increase the amount of mito-chondria in your muscles by as much as 20 times." That means you can get your muscles to use oxygen more effectively, con-verting fuel molecules to the ATP that muscles need to contract, allowing your muscles to work harder, and longer.

Understanding how training affects your muscle fibers can help you decide how to train for your sport of choice. Jogging won't help your weight-lifting ability—although it will certainly improve your cardiovascular condition. When you are in good cardiovascular condition, your heart is good at delivering blood and its precious cargo of oxygen to your muscles and your muscles are good at extracting the oxygen from the blood. These things, in turn, improve your endurance. Lifting weights won't increase the endurance of a long-distance swimmer (although having strong quadriceps can help push a runner uphill).

While you can't really change your slow-twitch muscles to fast-twitch or vice versa, you can improve the workings of both. Building up mitochondria in fast-twitch muscles makes them more able to withstand longer exercise. According to Jim Ross, assistant coordinator of the adult fitness program at Ball State Labs in Indiana, "you can train fast-twitch to act more like slow-twitch," thereby increasing your endurance.

Why do my muscles sometimes burn when I'm exercising?

The "burn" comes from the build-up of lactic acid, which forms as a by-product of energy production by muscle fibers. As the fibers convert glycogen to ATP, some of the reactions take place without oxygen. In this process, a compound called *pyruvate* is produced.

Some of the pyruvate is absorbed into the muscle cell's mitochondria and converted into useful energy. But during strenuous exercise, the mitochondria can't handle all the pyruvate that's produced. The excess pyruvate becomes lactic acid, a dead end as far as energy production is concerned. As the concentration of lactic acid in the muscle fiber increases, the acidity of the cell changes, causing muscle fatigue and the all-too-familiar "burn."

The best way to relieve lactic-acid-induced soreness is to continue to move around, but at a slower pace and without strain or with massage. Both stimulate blood circulation, which cleans out the built-up lactic acid from the muscles.

Why do I feel sore the day after I exercise?

The soreness comes from inflammation of the muscles. If you overexercise or exercise improperly, you can make small tears in the muscle fibers. Various proteins and other material from inside the cell can then leak out. Your body's immune system sees the leaking material and tries to destroy it, creating a mild inflammation, which you feel as next-day soreness. (That's why taking anti-inflammatory drugs, like Advil, helps ease the pain.)

With training, your muscles get more resistant to exercise-induced stress and become less likely to tear or otherwise be damaged. According to Dr. Stephen Seiler, an exercise physiologist at the Institute of Sport and Health at Agder College in Kristiansand, Norway, "For the regular exerciser, next-day soreness is a sign of overstress and definitely should not happen every day or even very often."

The Aging and Gendered Muscle

The muscular changes that result from exercise are, alas, all too temporary. If you stop lifting weights, it only takes a few weeks for the muscles to go back to their old shape.

As you age, maintaining your muscles becomes even more difficult. That's partly because the body naturally begins to lose muscle mass after about the age of 30—sometimes by as much as six to seven pounds a decade. Lost muscle translates into lost strength (about one-third of all 74-year-old men and two-thirds of all 74-year-old women can't lift a gallon of milk), but it doesn't translate into lost weight.

That's because as the muscle cells shrink, the body stores excess energy as fat, which requires fewer calories to maintain. "Most people don't realize that even if they don't gain any weight, they'll get fat with age," says Pax Beale, who in 1995, at the age of 65, won the National Body Building Championship in the Men's Division. "You have to lift weights to keep the muscle mass up."

Unfortunately, the ability of the muscle to respond to exercise also decreases with age, which means an older person can exercise just as long and hard and not get the same effect as a younger person. Notes Dr. William Evans, an exercise physiologist and director of Noll Physiological Laboratories at Pennsylvania State University, "There's no

Pax Beale

question about it. People have to work harder to stay the same weight as they age."

Men tend to have more muscle mass than women, which is why they're better in weight-bearing sports, especially sports that require upper-body strength (they have 40 percent more of it than women do). Women have more fat and less muscle, which makes them good at endurance sports, like long-distance running and swimming. Physiologists aren't exactly sure why women do so well at long-distance running. (It may have to do with how women metabolize fat and carbohydrates to fuel their muscles.) In swimming, though, it seems clear that fat lends both buoyancy and insulation. In 1978, in fact, Penny Lee Dean swam the English Channel faster than any other woman—or *man*—had ever done before. (She held that record for 16 years.)

You Gotta Have Heart

Of course, any athlete—male or female—also has to work on that all-important muscle, the heart, by boosting cardio-vascular fitness.

Exercise improves your cardiovascular condition in a number of ways. First, and most simply, exercise improves your circulatory system both by creating more capillaries in the muscles, which helps distribute the blood to the mitochondria, and by increasing the size and elasticity of the 60,000 miles of arteries and veins that course through your body.

Second, exercise can increase the *cardiac output* of the heart, which is the volume of blood that each ventricle of your heart can pump in a minute. A normal man's cardiac output is about five liters per minute, when he's standing still. When he exercises it rises to about 20, 30, even 35 liters a minute. Habitual exercise makes the heart get larger (it's a muscle after all), which means it can consistently pump more blood.

The more you exercise, the larger your heart gets, and the more blood it can pump. In fact, elite athletes often develop large hearts, called "athlete hearts" (as do elite canine athletes, like sled dogs), which pump extraordinary amounts of blood. (This efficiency also makes an athlete's resting heart rate drop. The average resting heart rate for a healthy adult is 72 beats per minute; a good athlete's often drops into the 40s and 50s.)

Lungs are crucial to the cardiovascular system too; after all, they bring in the oxygen. Regular exercise helps improve the whole body's efficiency at using that oxygen. One way of measuring cardiovascular health is measuring how much oxygen your body can consume when you are exercising, a measurement called maximal oxygen consumption or "$VO_{2\,max}$."

What happens to my heart when I exercise?

When you exercise, your heart has to pump more blood to supply oxygen to your muscles. The volume of blood that your heart pumps in a minute depends on the heart rate (the number of beats per minute) and the stroke volume (the blood volume pumped by each ventricle of your heart with each beat).

When you exercise, your heart beats faster and contracts more forcefully, pushing out more blood and increasing its stroke volume. During vigorous exercise, the return of blood from your veins to your heart increases, causing the ventricles of your heart to fill more fully with blood, stretching them a bit. Like other muscles, the heart contracts more forcefully if it is stretched a little before contraction. So the increase in returning blood also adds to the stoke volume by increasing the volume of blood in each ventricle and by causing the heart to beat more forcefully.

By training aerobically on a regular basis, you gradually increase the volume of blood that your heart can pump in a minute. This change results from an increase in your heart's stroke volume, since the maximum heart rate isn't changed by training.

What is "VO$_{2\,max}$" and how does it measure cardiovascular fitness?

One way to determine how fit you are is to measure how much oxygen your body can efficiently consume—a measurement of how hard your muscles are working. Your VO$_{2\,max}$ is the measurement of how much oxygen you consume in a minute, while exercising at sea level. The greater your oxygen consumption, the better your cardiovascular health.

Hospital fitness programs measure a person's VO$_{2\,max}$ by having a person exercise under conditions that push the heart's ability to deliver blood to its maximum. For instance, you might run on a treadmill that increases in speed and/or steepness at regular intervals. While you are exercising, you breathe out through sensors that measure air volume and oxygen concentration. Computer analysis determines how much oxygen your body is using. As the workload increases, so does your oxygen consumption—up to a point. At that point, exercising harder shifts the muscles into anaerobic activity. Soon after this point, the muscles will fatigue and you will have to stop exercising.

VO$_{2\,max}$ can be expressed as an absolute number—the number of liters of oxygen a person consumes in a minute. Or it can be expressed as a relative number—the number of milliliters of oxygen a person consumes in a minute divided by the person's weight in kilograms.

The average relative VO$_{2\,max}$ of an untrained man in his mid-30s is about 40–45 ml/min/kg. After an endurance exercise program, that same man might have a VO$_{2\,max}$ of 50–55 ml/min/kg. An Olympic champion 10,000 meter runner might have a value approaching or over 80 ml/min/kg. And if you think jockeys just get to go along for the ride while their horses do all the work, think again. One study found that a jockey's VO$_{2\,max}$ can be as high as 69 ml/min/kg.

How much exercise do you need to change your body in this way? Different experts give different answers. In 1993, the U.S. Centers for Disease Control and Prevention and the American College of Sports Medicine claimed that sweating, heavy breathing, and pumping iron weren't really necessary for fitness. Instead, the report claimed, Americans could reap benefits through spurts of mild "physical activity," including vacuuming, laundry, gardening, and walking, throughout the day. In 1996, a Surgeon General's report echoed the same theme.

That may sound appealing, but experts agree that more exercise really does more for your body. Jogging (5–8 miles per hour) for 20 to 30 minutes will help your heart more than doing the laundry. Running more may have even greater benefits. In a survey of readers of *Runner's World,* Dr. Paul Williams of Lawrence Berkeley Laboratory found that most indicators of coronary heart disease—including cholesterol levels and blood pressure—showed improvements up through 50 miles of running a week. Forty other studies have found similar findings.

Keeping up the exercise as we age can be crucial. A 1995 LBL study found that both low-mileage male runners (those who run less than 10 miles per week) and high-mileage runners (those who run more than 50 miles per week) will gain about the same weight and inches around their waist. But men who increase their weekly distance by at least 1.3 miles with each passing birthday can offset that increase in waist circumference. Since men and women with male pattern obesity (more commonly known as "the tire around the middle") are at high risk for heart attacks, the extra effort is worth it.

Most exercise physiologists recommend a bare minimum of 30 minutes a day of aerobic exercise, no matter how old you are. "There's really no evidence that aerobic exercise, for instance, wears out the knees," says Evans. "The real problem is when someone who is 40 or 50 years old decides to get back all he has lost since he was 20 and trains too hard all at once. That's where injuries happen." What about all that stuff about getting exercise by vacuuming and weeding the garden? It doesn't really get your heart rate up, but it helps burn calories, which, over the long run, can help keep your weight down.

The Shadow Side

Exercise is good—but can you exercise too much? Is it possible to be too fit?

Perhaps the fittest athletes around are today's Olympians. Back when the first modern Olympics were held in 1896, few of the competitors were full-time athletes. The 1896 Olympic ranks included an opera star, a foundry worker, a clerk, and a mailman. Thirty years later, most athletes still lived fairly modest lives. American George Roth, in fact, was unemployed during the 1932 Olympics in Los Angeles. After he won his gold medal, he had to hitchhike back to his home in East Hollywood.

But these days, corporate sponsorships have made it possible to be a full-time athlete, training 20, 30, or 40 hours a week (the rest of us are lucky if we get in four hours a week). Gary Hall, Jr., for instance, swims six hours a day, covering some seven miles in the pool. Dan O'Brien, the decathlon gold medalist in the 1996 Olympics, lifts weights every day, and then alternates running,

Do you drink enough water when you exercise?

Take this true-false quiz to find out.
True or false:

1   When you are exercising, you should drink when you get thirsty.

2   You should drink at least a quart of water for every hour you work out.

3   If you are exercising in a hot climate and you aren't used to the heat, you need to drink more than someone who is.

4   Your sweat can provide nutrition for 65,000 bacteria per square inch of skin—and that's a good thing!
(Answers on page 25.)

long jump, high jump, and shot-put three days a week, with discus, pole vault, javelin, and hurdles two days a week. Dot Richardson, of the U.S. softball team, trains 30 hours each week, including jogging, sprints, and doing 220 pounds on the leg press.

This pursuit of an athletic ideal is admirable, even awesome. But sometimes the pursuit of the perfect body goes too far. Some athletes train so hard, for example, they upset their bodies' natural functioning. Others choose to ingest, inject, or otherwise imbibe foreign substances to boost their performance.

Overdevelopment of a tennis player's arm is known as "King Kong arm."

Girl gymnasts, for instance, train so intensively at early ages that they suppress vital hormonal changes and practically defy puberty. Ordinarily, a girl's body starts producing estrogen in earnest between the ages of 8 to 10. Estrogen production increases over the next 5 to 10 years, stimulating the normal teenage growth spurt, and then it reaches a plateau. Intense training suppresses that estrogen production, with results that are obvious if you look at most 17-, 18-, or 19-year-old gymnasts. At an age where many females have developed a woman's body and a woman's reproductive abilities, these "older" gymnasts still look like prepubescent girls.

Lack of estrogen has a hidden cost as well. Estrogen affects bone density, so having abnormally low levels puts these gymnasts at risk for spinal problems, growth stunting, and bone fractures during their teen-aged years. In later years, former gymnasts may also have more trouble with osteoporosis.

Male gymnasts don't need to starve themselves or stave off puberty because they benefit from the upper-body strength conferred by rising levels of testosterone in their systems, which occurs with the onset of puberty. Football, basketball, and soccer players enjoy the same change. Indeed, the effect is so noticeable that many athletes, rather than struggling to become hormonally challenged, become hormonally enhanced with steroids.

Steroid use began in the 1930s, when Nazi doctors started giving steroids to soldiers to see if it would make them more aggressive in battle. Soviet officials began giving steroids to

Side Effects of Steroid Use

In teenage boys, testosterone triggers the production of a growth hormone, which causes a growth spurt. Testosterone also stimulates synthesis of proteins, which, in turn, results in increased muscle mass.

In an attempt to increase their muscle mass and strength, some athletes use testosterone-like agents called *anabolic steroids*. Unfortunately, men and women using steroids have experienced multiple side effects, some of which are illustrated below.

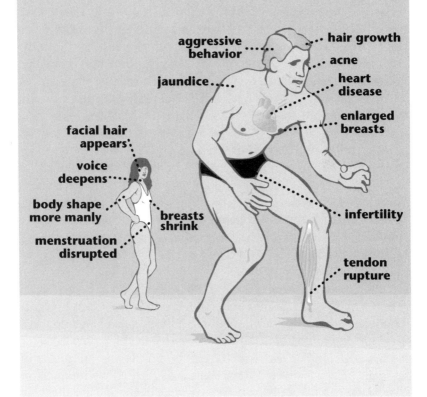

aggressive behavior

hair growth

acne

jaundice

heart disease

enlarged breasts

facial hair appears

voice deepens

body shape more manly

breasts shrink

menstruation disrupted

infertility

tendon rupture

athletes; other countries followed suit. Today, "drug use is epidemic in high-level sports, and it has been for a long time," says Dr. Charles Yesalis, an epidemiologist at Pennsylvania State University and author of *Anabolic Steroids in Sports and Exercise.* The most common are testosterone-based anaerobic steroids, which increase bone and muscle mass, while reducing fat and boosting the blood's oxygen-carrying capacity. In men, that translates into increased muscles, weight gain, endurance, and power. Women reap the same benefits; they also acquire male traits like a deepened voice, and tough skin.

Steroids are just part of a larger problem. Athletes can take hundreds of different kinds of drugs, including human growth hormone (a genetically engineered version of the natural substance that helps make bones and muscles grow in children) and "Epo" (a version of the hormone erythropoetin, which speeds the body's red cell production to five or even ten times normal rate). Red blood cells transport oxygen from the lungs to the rest of the body; increasing the number of red blood cells helps transport more oxygen to the muscles, which essentially gives the muscles more fuel.

Athletes have also made use of caffeine; the International Olympic Committee now bans caffeine levels that are more than the equivalent of about six cups of coffee. But one of the oddest cases of substance abuse was cited in a *Village Voice* story about Steve Michalik, who held the titles of both Mr. America and Mr. World. He claimed that at one point he cracked open a monkey's skull and drank fluid from its hypothalamus. Dr. Yesalis wasn't surprised to hear this. "My colleagues and I like to joke that if we wrote an article saying people are drinking donkey urine and it's beneficial, people would start doing it," he says. "People are just so hungry for an edge."

The problem is that most of these substances can be very dangerous. Cyclists and runners have been creating Epo effects for years by injecting themselves with their own blood (called blood doping), with mixed results. But using Epo can make the blood too thick for the heart to handle. "There are reports that a number of athletes in Europe who have suffered from sudden deaths during competition were on Epo," Dr. Yesalis says. "It turns your blood into a slurpy."

Sustained use of steroids can damage the heart and liver, cause sterility, and induce what weight lifters call "'roid rage," or aggression and delusions. (Michalik claims that while he was on steroids his testicles shrank to the size of peanuts, he had chronic nosebleeds, he developed a grapefruit-sized liver tumor, and his cholesterol count was a whopping 500. According to the National Institutes of Health, a desirable cholesterol count is less than 200.)

Despite these problems, estimates of the number of athletes who use steroids are shockingly high. In 1990, the Atlanta Falcon's Bill Fralic claimed some 75 percent of the NFL's linemen, linebackers, and tight ends had used steroids. Notes Beale, "if you look at the average size of linemen in the NFL and the NCAA, you have to ask what's going on. Why is everyone getting so big?" A 1993 study at the University of Alabama found that the mean weight of even high school football players has increased from 213 pounds in 1963 to 268 pounds in 1989. One possible cause of this could be the use of steroids, which, in young men, could result in premature skeletal maturation, decreased sperm count, and increased risk of injury.

Steve Michalik, who was both Mr. America and Mr. World, claims that while he was on steroids his testicles shrank to the size of peanuts. And his cholesterol count was a whopping 500.

Testing is increasing too; for the 1996 Olympics, in fact, the IOC spent more than three million dollars to test for drug use. But "every time testing makes a stride, the users are a stride and a half in front of it," Dr. Yesalis says. "They develop new drugs long before the officials develop tests for them or they learn to get around the existing tests. I could teach you how to disguise steroid use in about two minutes." The potential dangers won't discourage users, he says, because "there's just too much at stake, in terms of money, to let someone else get the advantage. Drugs sell the Olympic business. People don't pay to watch the world's 151st fastest time in the 100-meter dash. They pay to see world records broken."

Physicist Party Trick

Test Your Reaction Time

Exploratorium physicist Paul Doherty is master of many strange tricks. (Perhaps you saw him on "Late Night with David Letterman." He was the one sitting on a frictionless disk and propelling himself across the stage with a fire extinguisher.)

The Exploratorium physicists often claim educational value for tricks we are certain they learned just because they are cool. Here's one of Paul's favorites.

Like to make bets you know you'll win? Challenge your friends to catch a dropped dollar bill (if you feel particularly daring, go for a twenty). If they can grab it, they can keep it. If they miss, it's yours.

Here are the rules. Your friend rests his arm on the edge of a table or chair, with the hand hanging over the edge. Your friend holds his thumb and index finger about an inch apart while you place the dollar bill in the middle between the fingers, with the portrait of George Washington (or, for the daring, Andrew Jackson) level with the fingers. Then, without warning, you drop the dollar bill.

Try as he might, your friend probably won't be able to close his fingers fast enough to catch the bill. That's because, for most people, it takes almost two tenths of a second for the fingers to respond to the brain's command to close. But it takes much less time for the dollar bill to slip through their fingers.

You can measure your reaction time if you do essentially the same thing with a yardstick instead of a dollar bill. Rest your arm on the edge of a table or chair, with your hand hanging over the edge (this prevents you from dropping your hand down to match the yardstick's motion). Hold your thumb and index finger about an inch apart, and have a friend hold a yardstick so that its end is just between the two fingers. Without warning, have them drop the yardstick and, as fast as you can, close your fingers on the stick.

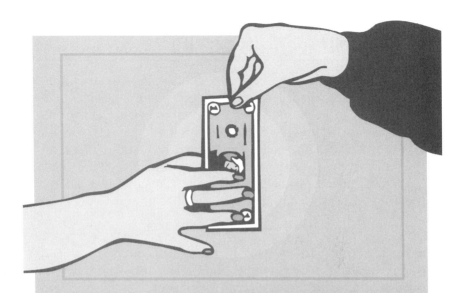

Note the inch reading where your fingers hold the stick. For most people, about six inches will have fallen through before they can grab the yardstick. Now do you see why the party trick always works? You're only giving your friend about three inches of dollar bill to try to catch, about half of what they need. They never had a chance.

If you want to convert the distance the yardstick fell to a reaction time, use the following table:

Inches Fallen	Reaction Time (sec)
5	0.161
5.5	0.169
6	0.177
6.5	0.184
7	0.191
7.5	0.198
8	0.204
8.5	0.210

You Gotta Have Heart Part II

Of course, many athletes deal with bodily deficiencies without using drugs. Although size is often considered a pre-eminent concern, many athletes manage to overcome being the "wrong" height. At six feet tall, Bobby Jennings is the tallest jockey ever to ride in the United States. He didn't often ride small horses, and spectators recognized him by how high his butt lifted off the saddle, but he was one of the leading jockeys in California in the 1960s. (He weighed between 110 and 118 while he was a jockey; he now weighs 170).

George Mikan, by comparison, was the first really big guy to make it in basketball—at 6'10", he was at first considered too darn clumsy to play the game. But his smart coach at DePaul University recognized and nurtured Mikan's latent talent. The big man went on to become one of pro basketball's first stars in the late 1940s, thereby paving the way for the giant men who dominate the game today.

Many athletes also overcome what can be the limiting factor of age. Although Olympic gymnasts and divers seem to be getting younger and younger, consider Bill Shoemaker, one of the best jockeys in history. He raced until he was 58, and George Foreman won the heavyweight championship at age 45. Both of these men have excelled athletically at an age when most people, even athletes, have begun to rest on past laurels.

Whatever the limitations and whatever the means of overcoming them, the moral seems pretty clear. Having a good body helps. Having real heart may help more.

Do you drink enough water when you exercise?

Here are the answers to the questions on page 17.

1 False. Actually you need to start drinking *before* you get thirsty. You can lose as much as two quarts of water before thirst kicks in. If you weigh 150 pounds, two quarts of water is 2.6% of your body weight. A water loss equal to just one percent of your body weight is enough to affect your exercise performance. If you don't have enough water in your system, your body's cooling mechanisms—sweating and blood flow to the skin—become less efficient and you fatigue quicker. When you are dehydrated, you may feel tired and stressed out after a workout, rather than feeling energetic and relaxed. You may have a headache and feel sick to your stomach.

2 More or less true. How much you need to drink depends on how much you sweat. A quart of water is a good start—but you may need more. In very strenuous activity, people have been know to lose as much as four quarts of sweat in an hour. If you want to know for sure how much water you need to drink, weigh yourself naked before exercising, then weigh yourself again after exercising. For every pound you lost, you need to drink a pint of water.

3 False. If your body has adjusted to a hot climate, you will sweat more—which means you need to drink even more than someone who isn't used to the heat.

4 True. Your sweat provides nutrients for bacteria that live on the skin's surface. Those skin bacteria produce acidic waste products, which make the skin's surface acidic. This acidity protects you from other harmful bacteria that might otherwise take up residence on your skin.

2 Bodies in Motion

WHEN BARON Pierre de Coubertin established the modern Olympic Games in 1896, he chose the Latin motto *"Citius, altius, fortius,"* or "swifter, higher, stronger." People continue to bring that motto alive as every year passes. Records for speed, distance, and weight have been made and broken again and again this century (no one kept track before 1896). In fact, as of 1996, no athletic record established before 1980 still stands. We may have gone only a thousandth of an inch farther or a thousandth of a second faster, but we're continuing to push the envelope, little bit by little bit.

Are humans actually getting stronger and faster? It hardly seems likely, given the highly mechanized nature of today's society. But our abilities to use technology to analyze and boost performance are racing forward at awesome speeds. The question is: when will we reach our peak? What's the fastest a human body can run, swim, or fly through the air?

Walking the Walk

Let's start with the simplest steps first. Have you ever wondered how a human walks? Your body actually works like an inverted pendulum—with your torso swinging above your planted legs like the ticker on a grandfather clock. When you walk, your torso doesn't swing at a smooth or steady pace. As you lift your foot, you're fighting gravity, so your pace slows slightly. As your foot swings down again, the pace speeds up slightly, and you store enough energy to use to push off again. Each time you place your feet, your body shifts forward slightly.

By the time you've mastered walking, you've probably learned to first place one foot only so far in front of your body, then to move your body only so far in front of your planted foot, and then to bring your trailing foot forward fast enough to catch you before you fall flat on your face. For adults, walking feels totally natural; we hardly even notice what we're doing. But anyone who has seen a toddler start to toddle knows that this constant lifting, placing, and shifting is no mean feat.

The toddler's problem isn't just learning to balance—first on two little platforms way down there on the ground, and then on one at a time (as she moves her feet). It's also learning to coordinate the natural up-and-down movement that comes as we roll from heel to toe with the side-to-side movement that comes as we rotate our hips.

Chimpanzees swagger like cowhands, because they swivel each hip around the supporting leg.

This is one way that humans are a bit more evolved than chimpanzees. The reason chimps swagger like cowhands is because they haven't quite gotten that up-and-down movement down yet. Instead, the chimps swivel their hips around the supporting leg with each step. They flail their arms about because they need them for balance; a chimp's center of gravity is higher on its spine than a human's is, which makes a chimp slightly top heavy. That's actually better for swinging through trees (in what's called "suspensory motion"), but it's not so great for standing tall or striding across the plains.

Running Away

The difference between running and walking is that when you run you lose contact with the ground. Each stride makes you airborne, because your muscles act like springs or pogo sticks. As your foot lands on the ground and your leg sinks downward, it stores energy in the tendons. When you push off from the ground again, the energy releases, bouncing you back up in the air.

The best bouncers in the world are kangaroos, which have long legs, long feet, and long Achilles tendons for storing energy. As the kangaroo jumps, it pushes off on its tiptoes, extending its legs. When the kangaroo lands, its legs bend and it stores energy in its tendons for the next bounce. Running humans land on one foot at a time, but kangaroos use both hind feet at the same time, so they get double the bounce for the buck—a gray kangaroo, in fact, can travel more than 20 feet in one bound!

"Depends on how far my refrigerator is."

—George Foreman, asked about how far he runs in training

But in humans, running doesn't just involve the legs; it also involves the arms. Swinging your right arm forward as your left leg moves back when you are jogging feels entirely natural; so does pumping your arms when you need to sprint across a busy street or chug up a long hill. That's because swinging your arms downward gives you more power when you push off from the ground with the opposite leg. (Raising the opposite thigh helps too.) This works because of Newton's third law of motion: for every action there is an equal and opposite reaction. In this case, the harder you pump your arms (that's the action) the harder you can shove off from the ground (that's the reaction).

Over the years, it seems runners have made that action-reaction pattern go faster and faster. Only sixty years ago, no one thought we would ever run faster than a four-minute mile. But Sir Roger Bannister broke that barrier in 1954. Today's record is 3:44.39 for men and 4:15.61 for women.

The 100-meter record time has fallen steadily too. In 1896, the record was 12 seconds flat. Jesse Owens ran it in 10.3 seconds in 1936. Since then the time has plummeted to Jim Hines's 9.95 in 1968, Leroy Burrell's 9.85 in 1995, and Donavan Bailey's 9.84 in 1996. The best time for the 200 meter has dropped from Jesse Owen's 20.7 in 1936 to Michael Johnson's 19.32 in 1996, a time most statisticians didn't expect to see for several decades. Even amateur athletes are getting better: in the spring of 1996, Bertha Holt, a 92-year-old grandmother from Oregon, set a world Master's record for the 400 meter: 3:45.62.

Why are runners getting faster? The records changes are, at least in part, due to our increased understanding of the finer points of biomechanics, which has resulted in changes in training and techniques. For instance, most runners used to avoid weight training for fear of "getting bunched up." Now most do at least some weight training to get more explosive power in their quads and hamstrings and to develop upper-body strength.

Technique changes include the one pioneered by Edwin Moses. In 1976, Moses realized that taking 13 steps, rather than 14 steps, between hurdles contributed to his gold medal at the Olympics. Today, "everyone tries to do 13 strides, because they know it's optimal. But not everyone can," says Hal Bateman, the historian and statistician for USA Track and Field, the national governing body for such events.

Similarly, our understanding of stride mechanics is evolving. In the late 1980s, Bob Prichard, director of Somax Posture and Sport Science in Corte Madera, California, found that the "stride angle," or the angle between the front and trailing leg, has a big effect on speed. When he analyzed male runners in the 1988 Olympics, he found that "in every single race, the top four finished in order of their stride angle." Sometimes, Prichard says, "it was only a difference of 1 or 2 degrees. But every degree increase in stride angle translates to a 2 degree difference in stride length." Put all those differences in stride length together, Prichard says, and you can shave a full second off a one-mile run.

Cheetahs are a good example of animals with big stride angle. In the cheetah's case, the stride comes from its flexible back and shoulders. These allow it to move its back feet in front of its front feet, which allows it to whip across the plains at a sizzling 60 miles per hour. That's one reason a cheetah can complete the 400-meter race in 16 seconds, compared with a little more than 43 seconds for very athletic humans.

Equipment also plays a large role in record breaking. When Jesse Owens won his four gold medals at the 1936 Olympics in Berlin (three were for running in the 100-meter, 200-meter, and 4 × 100 relay; the fourth was for the long jump), his shoes were leather and probably weighed several pounds. Today's sprinter's shoes are made of leather and synthetic materials, weigh only a few ounces, and are often custom designed for the runner's feet. Such shoes can shave as much as one second per lap off a runner's time. Marathoners wear microchips in their shoelaces so they can time the pace of their long races exactly.

Even modern track surfaces help athletes run faster. Until the 1970s, most sprinters ran on cinders, hard dirt, or even concrete. Today, researchers have developed a number of running surface materials that are custom designed for each distance. Sprinters, for instance, require track surfaces that are springy enough to return a maximum amount of bounce to a runner's foot, but not so soft that the foot gets bogged down on contact. Long distance runners need a softer surface, one that absorbs more of the energy of the impact, so that the runners' leg muscles and ligaments aren't jolted too much with every step.

Tracks can make enough of a difference to result in some controversy when records are broken. When Carl Lewis broke the 100-meter record in Tokyo in 1991, some critics complained that the super-hard track in Tokyo helped him shave that crucial four-hundreths of a second off the previous record.

No matter how fast we get though, we'll probably forever be slowpokes compared with some of our fellow creatures. A cheetah can accelerate from 0 to 70 miles per hour in three seconds. But based on the number of steps per second, the fastest creature on earth is the American cockroach, which can take 50 steps per second. If a cockroach were the size of a person, that pace would carry it forward at a good 220 miles per hour. Do you think that's an unfair comparison because a cockroach has six legs? When the little bugger gets going that fast, it actually rears onto its two back legs and becomes bipedal.

Fishes We Ain't

Humans really aren't the best swimmers in the world either. A sailfish can swim as fast as 65 miles per hour, but most humans swim at just under 5 mph.

Water is 773 times denser and 55 times more viscous than air. To move through the water, a swimmer has to push all that heavy water aside. So it's not surprising that swimming burns energy at four times the rate of running; swimming two miles is like running eight. To double your speed through the water, you have to put out eight times as much power; to increase it by even 10 percent calls for 30 percent more effort.

Swimming is tough because humans create a tremendous amount of "form drag" in the water. "Drag" is the resistance created by water flowing around the body and creating a turbulent wake behind it. How much drag there is depends on a number of factors, including the speed of the object, the size of the area facing forward, and the shape and smoothness of the object. Skiers and bikers tuck up into a semi-curled position because it reduces the "frontal area" they present to the wind. Swimmers can't tuck (they wouldn't go anywhere), but they can try to keep themselves as streamlined as possible.

If you took swimming lessons as a kid, your teacher probably told you not to kick too hard. The main purpose of kicking is to keep your legs up, which helps reduce drag. Legs only account for 20 percent of the power of a swimmer; a full 80 percent of swimming power comes from the arms.

Like running times, swimming times are getting faster. In 1928, Johnny Weissmuller (who, later, as the movies' Tarzan, learned to swim with a knife in his mouth) became the first man to swim 100 meters in less than a minute; it was a decade before anyone beat his time. Weissmuller was also one of the first swimmers to take a breath with every stroke, instead of every fourth or sixth stroke. (In 1928, the Japanese filmed him to deconstruct his gold medal technique in the crawl. At the Los Angeles Olympics in 1932, the Japanese made use of what they learned and won all but one swimming event.)

Swimming technique has come a long way since our Tarzan sliced through the Olympic pools. Changes in technique have played the biggest role in speeding up swimmers. Swimmers' hand positions, for example, have changed radically. Before 1970, most swimmers tried to keep their hands straight, like canoe paddles, as they pulled them through the water in the freestyle. But this is hard to do—the arm and hand naturally want to wiggle a bit as they go through the water. As it turns out, it's more efficient to allow a little wiggling. In the early 1970s, swimming coach Ernest Maglischo figured out that moving the hand in an S-shaped pattern creates extra lift by making it work like a propeller.

What's the best position for my hands when I swim freestyle?

If you learned to swim before the mid-1970s (and maybe later, depending on the coach), you were probably taught to pull your hand straight backward through the water like a canoe paddle. With this stroke, you move forward by pushing against the water. It turns out that's *not* the best way to propel yourself through the water. Today's swimmers learn to follow an S-shaped pattern (see diagram below), a more natural motion that has more in common with a propeller than a paddle.

With the S-shaped motion, the edge of your hand splits the water flowing past it into two streams, much like what happens when an airplane wing cuts through the air. Some water goes over the back of your hand and some goes under it. This split generates a lift, which propels you forward in the water, similar to the way a propeller's wing-shaped blades push a boat forward.

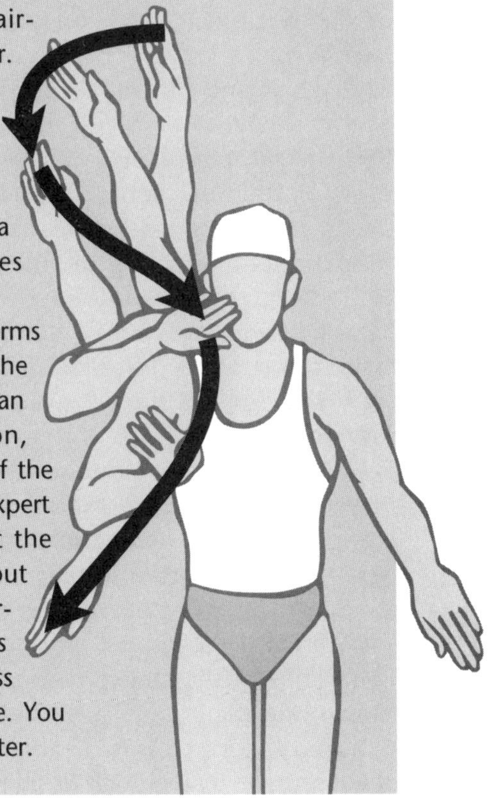

We tend to think of lift in terms of moving you upward (as is the case with an airplane), but lift can be generated in any direction, depending on the orientation of the hand (or wing) that creates it. Expert swimmers continuously adjust the angle of their hands throughout the stroke to maximize the forward-directed lift. This lift means a swimmer can go faster with less effort using the S-shaped stroke. You can almost "fly" through the water.

Other researchers are working on the patterning and timing of shoulder and hip rotation. Moving the hips and the shoulders has two effects: it helps generate more power in the arms and legs and it helps reduce drag. "We're finding that rolling the shoulders during the crawl stroke helps to reduce the swimmer's frontal area surface," says Jane Cappaert, director of bio-mechanics for U.S. Swimming, the national governing body for swimming events. "With one shoulder out of the water, the body works like the bottom of a boat. When both shoulders are flat, the body is more like a barge. It creates more resistance."

In their efforts to determine how fish swim so efficiently, engineers at Massachusetts Institute of Technology have constructed a robotic replica of a bluefin tuna that they call RoboTuna.

Bob Prichard, the fellow who analyzed runners' stride angles, has also been working on hip rotation. After analyzing elite male swimmers at the University of California, Berkeley, Prichard discovered that most of their swimming power in the freestyle and backstroke comes from hip rotation, not arm pull. This could be pretty revolutionary stuff. Even top swimmers tend to ignore hip rotation, letting it follow each arm stroke naturally. But Prichard has found that deliberately rotating the hips can lend astounding power to a swimmer's stroke.

"Actually, when I analyzed Matt Biondi, who was then the fastest swimmer in the world, I found that he had 10 percent less power in his arms than other swimmers," Prichard says. "But he had 70 percent more power in his hips."

Elite swimmers, like Biondi and Alexander Popov, Prichard says, have a 60-degree rotation in their hips, although "they don't know what they're doing." Other swimmers can learn to isolate and then increase and efficiently use their hip rotation, by using special belts and pulleys. That can increase the power of each stroke by as much as 20 percent, Prichard says.

Like Fishes in the Sea

Swimmers are working on other techniques too. One of the most novel may be that of Misty Hyman, a 17-year-old from Phoenix. Hyman read a *Scientific American* article that described how fishes use their tails to reduce drag. According to research, a submarine the size and shape of a dolphin would need seven times as much power to swim at the speed a dolphin swims. Biologists theorize that the flexible movement of a dolphin creates vortices or eddies in the water. The dolphin pushes off these vortices with its tail. By pushing off these vortices, the dolphin reclaims energy that would otherwise be wasted, and therefore swims more efficiently.

In 1936, zoologist James Gray calculated that a dolphin was too weak, by a factor of about seven, to swim as fast as it did. Scientists are still working out the details of how dolphins and fish swim so efficiently.

Hyman and her coach, Bob Gillett, worked out an analogous human fish kick, in which Hyman dives into the water, turns sideways, and then, putting her arms straight over her head like a torpedo and keeping her legs together, kicks them from side to side. Though she didn't qualify for the March 1996 Olympic trials, that May she beat all of the Olympic butterfliers—including Amy Van Dyken, who went on to win the gold in Atlanta.

Hyman's novel technique may revolutionize butterfly times; it may also disqualify her from competition. If a technique is too innovative, the rules may be changed to outlaw it. In 1956, Masaru Furukawa of Japan set an Olympic record in the breast-stroke when he swam 75 percent of the way underwater, thus provoking a ban on swimming underwater for more than 15 meters.

Changes in equipment have also helped swimmers increase their speed. A swimmer moving through the water experiences what's called surface drag—water sticks to the swimmer and forms an adhesive boundary layer. Modern swimmers shave their body hair to reduce surface drag. Some say shaving has resulted in a speed increase of about one second in the men's 100-meter freestyle. Tighter bathing suits also help reduce surface drag and turbulence around the body. In fact, swimmers now wear synthetic suits that are smoother than human skin. Jon Henricks, the Australian who won the gold medal for the 100-meter freestyle in the 1956 Olympics, pioneered this trend in 1952, when he wore a silk suit that his mother sewed from women's lingerie.

Even an equipment change as simple as goggles can have an effect. Because goggles reduce eye irritation, swimmers can train longer.

Olympic pools also now have wave-damping devices— including gutters along the pool and foam lane dividers—that reduce the drag and turbulence confronting swimmers. It wasn't always so comfortable. In the 1920 Olympics in Antwerp, swimmers jumped into the dark water of a moat that surrounded the city. The water was only 52 degrees and rats joined the competition. (In fact, some people claimed that the rats swam faster than the humans.)

World swimming records continue to drop. Between 1921 and 1976, alone, in fact, the women's record for the 400-meter freestyle dropped from 6:16.6 to 4:11.69—more than two full minutes. Is there a limit to the speed? "There are still faster speeds to go," Cappaert says. "But how much faster is debatable. No one's making any predictions."

They Fly through the Air

Humans are no more suited to flying through the air than to swimming rapidly through the water, but oh how we love to hurl ourselves through the light stuff. To stay aloft for any length of time, we need to generate lift—the same force that keeps an airplane aloft. To do that we need to be moving fast. But there's a catch: the faster we go, the more drag we encounter. In fact, aerodynamic drag increases in proportion to the square of the speed. In other words, a moving object experiences four times more drag at 20 miles per hour than it did at 10 miles per hour.

To fly as far as possible, you need a good lift-drag ratio. That is, you want the biggest possible lift and the smallest possible drag.

Ski jumping is a good example of how a person can reduce drag while enhancing lift. A ski jumper crouches down low as he zips down the ramp at a good 23 meters per second (about 45 miles per hour). This position reduces drag, allowing him to go fast, and puts him in a position to push off at takeoff. Twenty meters from the end of the ramp and less than one second before takeoff, "he catapults his body forward over the ski tips," says Joe Lamb, who competed in the 1972 Olympics and coached the 1984 Olympic ski jumping team.

In this position, the jumper's body and skis form an aerodynamic shape that generates lift as he speeds through the air. This position also reduces drag, so that the jumper can "fly" a long way.

In the late 1980s, ski jumpers developed a technique that significantly enhanced the aerodynamic properties of their jumps. By placing their skis in a V—with the front tips spread apart and the tail ends touching—"they increased aerodynamic lift by about 36 percent," Lamb says, "while reducing drag by about 30 percent." So the change in technique allowed jumpers to "fly" for even further distances on the same courses.

That's all well and good, unless you worry about jumpers

How high can you jump?

Next time you watch a basketball or volleyball game, notice how high the athletes jump to block a shot or spike the ball. Ever wonder if you could jump as high? Here's a simple way to find out, courtesy of the Exploratorium's own physicist/athlete/all-around-nice-guy Paul Doherty.

Stand next to a wall with a short pencil in your hand and hold your arm as high above your head as you can, keeping your feet flat on the floor. Make a mark on the wall to note your standing reach. Then jump as high as you can, keeping your arm high above your head. At the top of your jump, make another mark on the wall. It works best to stand close to, but not touching, the wall when you jump. The difference in height between the two marks is a measure of how high you jumped.

You may be able to jump higher if you change how much you bend your knees before jumping. As you straighten your knees, you push your feet harder into the floor, which allows you to push off the ground with more force and jump higher. If you don't bend your knees much, you don't get much extra push. On the other hand, a deep crouch overstretches the thigh muscles, making them less efficient in pushing you off the ground. Experiment to find the amount of knee bend that gives you the most height.

Swinging your arms up can also add to your jump's height. As your arms swing up, your body is forced downward in reaction, increasing the force with which you push off the ground, and, therefore, the height of your jump. To be effective, your arms must finish their upward motion before your feet leave the ground.

This method of measuring a person's vertical jump is known as a Sargent jump, after Dudley Sargent, one of the pioneers in American physical education. When he studied a group of college students early in this century, he found that, on average, they jumped about 20 inches. There are no official records for a jump like this, but in 1976, basketball player Darrell Griffith's standing vertical jump measured four feet!

Why do long jumpers "run" several steps in the air after they take off?

The hitch-kick, as the running motion is called, stops the forward rotation of the jumper's body that he gets when he springs into the air. As the jumper plants his foot for takeoff, the motion of his lower body stops for the fraction of a second his foot is in contact with the board. But his upper body continues to move forward, which makes him start to rotate forward around his center of gravity. If unchecked, this rotation would send him face-down into the sand.

Long jumpers have learned to counteract this rotation by moving their hands and arms in the hitch-kick. During the hitch-kick, jumpers hold each leg straight as it moves backward and bent at the knees as it comes forward. This difference in leg position causes the jumper's lower body to move forward.

Similarly, the jumper's arm movements during the hitch-kick pushes the jumper's upper body backward. These body motions neutralize the takeoff rotation and allow the jumper to get into a better position for landing

When the jumper stops hitch-kicking, the takeoff rotation continues unchecked. The jumper rotates forward around a line that goes from side to side through his center of gravity. This rotation forces his legs (now stretched out in front of him) downward.

breaking their necks, which is part of the job of the ski jumping authorities. To counteract what could be some very fast, very long, and very dangerous jumps, the authorities changed other parameters of the sport. Lamb, who is now an executive board member of the International Ski Federation, says, "We're monitoring the takeoff velocity of the jumpers, as well as the wind elements," both of which can affect jump distance. "And we're evaluating the equipment on a yearly basis—for instance, ski length, width, and weight, as well as the fit, air permeability, and thickness of the jumping suits."

Hasn't anyone ever suggested banning the V-technique instead of making all those other changes instead? Absolutely not, Lamb says. "There's a difference between improvements brought about by human performance and improvements brought about by equipment. We should ban technological advancement, but we must allow changes in performace techniques to keep the sport improving in the eyes of the spectators and the media." All in all, he says, "the V-technique has actually made the sport a lot safer for the athlete."

Pole-vaulting is another way people fly through the air. A pole-vaulter uses the pole as a spring—when the jumper sprints up to the bar and plants the pole, he stores the energy of his motion in the pole. Then he drops his head backward and lifts first one leg, then both, making the pole bend far backwards over him. As he's hanging horizontal under the bowed pole, the stored energy is converted into vertical motion as the pole starts to give energy back. Then the jumper twists his body to get over the pole while pushing off from it with his arms.

Pole-vaulting technique hasn't changed much in the last 100 years. But the materials used for the pole itself have changed dramatically. Poles used to be made of bamboo, wood, or steel. But the fiberglass vaulting poles introduced in 1963 are far springier than the earlier materials. In 1960, the world record for pole-vaulting was 15 feet and it had increased by only a couple of inches in the previous 18 years. With the advent of fiberglass poles, records (and pole vaulters) started flying. By 1966, pole vaulters were flinging themselves more than 19 feet in the air. Today the record is 20'1.75".

One of the biggest controversies in the history of Olympic jumping occurred during the 1968 Olympics. The site of that year's Olympics, Mexico City, lies at 7000 feet, where the air is thinner—air pressure there is about 77 percent of the sea level value. That year, in the long jump event, Bob Beamon jumped an astounding 29'2.5" (2 feet farther than the previous record). A number of spoilsports said he was able to do this because of the thin air.

But according to Peter Brancazio, author of *SportsScience*, thin air wouldn't have given Beamon all that much of an edge. For the sprinting part of the jump, the thin air meant Beamon would have encountered 23 percent less drag than at sea level. That would have the same effect as a 1.4 meter-per-second trailing wind, which is still legal, and might have added about 1.5 inches to the length of his jump. Once Beamon was off the ground, the lower air resistance probably added about 2 inches to his jump. Brancazio also notes that Mexico City's elevation and location means that its gravity is .36 percent lower than the standard sea level value. The lower gravity in Mexico City might have added another inch to Beamon's jump. Combined, these factors could have added four-and-a-half inches to Beamon's jump—but he broke the record by two feet. So Beamon was a good jumper.

A flea can jump 130 times its height. If a human could do the same, the high jump record would be nearly 800 feet, high enough to carry the jumper over the Washington Monument with 250 feet to spare.

But some people are never satisfied. In Tokyo in 1991, at one of the first meets in which synthetic tracks were used, Mike Powell leapt 29'4.5", adding 2 inches to Beamon's record. A few critics said that Powell too had an unfair advantage when he tried to break the unfairly made previous world record: the harder synthetic track lent more speed to Powell's run.

Flop Physics

In 1968, Dick Fosbury won the Olympic gold medal in high jumping using a radical new jumping style in which he twisted his body at takeoff so that he jumped head first, his arched back toward the bar. He settled on this technique, now known as the Fosbury flop, after years of trial and error. He didn't know why it worked; he just knew it did. As more and more jumpers followed his example, coaches and scientists tried to figure out why it worked.

It turns out the secret is in the jumper's center of gravity. Everything—from a chair to a rabbit to a person—has a balance point, a point about which the weight on any one side is equal to the weight on the opposite side. If you stand with your hands at your sides, this balance point, called the *center of gravity* (or sometimes, the center of mass), is located in the middle of your

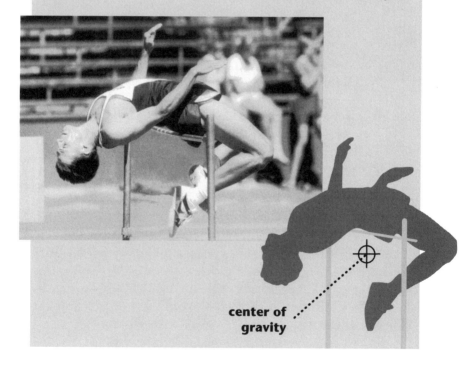

center of
gravity

body at a height that corresponds to 55 percent of your total height, measured from the floor; for most people, that's about one inch below their navel.

Changing your position changes the way your weight is distributed and therefore changes the location of your center of gravity. Raise your arms above your head, and your center of gravity rises several inches.

Depending on an object's shape, the center of gravity can even be located *outside* the object. The center of gravity of a donut, for example, is in the space at the center of its hole. Similarly, if you bend over at the waist, your hands reaching toward the ground, your center of gravity is now outside and in front of your body, within the "U" created by your arms and legs.

When you jump, you raise your center of gravity; an elite high jumper's center of gravity rises by more than four feet. It takes energy to raise your center of gravity; the higher you jump, the more energy you need. The goal of high jumpers is, therefore, to clear the bar while keeping their center of gravity as low as possible. To do this, they try to have as much of their body mass below the level of the bar at the peak of the jump as they can. The Fosbury flop, because of its exaggerated body arch, does this quite well.

At the peak, a "flopper's" center of gravity is outside of his body and under his arched back. If done just right, a flopper's center of gravity might even pass *under* the bar, while the jumper's body clears the bar cleanly. Jumpers who use other, less efficient styles (such as the straddle style) have to raise their centers of gravity several inches higher to clear the same height as a flopper does, and that's just plain harder to do. No wonder the new style caught on so quickly.

Spinning Out

Flying through the air doesn't always involve moving in a straight line. Gymnastics, figure skating, and high diving all depend on athletes' abilities to spin themselves in midair. These athletes make airborne spins look like the most natural thing in the world. But how do they do it?

To understand the biomechanics of spinning, you need to divide the body up by its axes. An axis is simply a line around which a body rotates. On the human body, the imaginary line from head to toe is called the longitudinal axis, or long axis. If you stand on the ground and spin around in a circle like a little kid trying to make himself dizzy, you're spinning around the long axis. The line from hip to hip is the transverse axis, or the short axis. Tuck your head and bring your knees up to do a somersault around that axis. Or you flip around this axis in midair with your body extended; that's called a layout. The line from front to back is the median axis. You rotate around that axis when you do a cartwheel on the ground or a "turntable" on the trampoline.

Humans control the speed of their spins by controlling how compact their bodies are. Picture a figure skater spinning on the ice. Usually she starts with her arms extended horizontally. When she brings her arms in close, she spins faster. Why? You might think it's because her arms created some kind of drag and folding them in reduced the drag. Good try. Instead, it's because of *angular momentum*, which is the tendency of a object that's spinning to keep spinning.

The amount of angular momentum depends on three things: an object's mass, its velocity, and the distance between the mass and the axis around which the object is rotating. You can calculate the angular momentum of a simple object with a simple equation: angular momentum equals the object's mass (m), multiplied by its velocity (v), multiplied by the distance between the mass and the axis around which it rotates (r). Or, as a physicist would write the equation: angular momentum = mvr.

For a complex object (like a human body), the distance from the mass and the axis is tough to calculate. What a physicist would do is consider the body as many small masses, then add together the angular momentum of each of those masses to get the total angular momentum for the object. But you don't need to do all that to get the basic idea.

The angular momentum of an object always stays the same unless you give the thing or the person a twist. Physicists call this principle the conservation of angular momentum.

When the figure skater brings her arms in, she reduces the distance between part of her mass (her arms) and her rotational axis (in this case the long axis). But her angular momentum has to stay the same; *mvr* has to equal the same number. Since the distance (*r*) has gotten smaller and her overall mass (*m*) hasn't changed, her velocity (*v*), the speed of her spin has to increase.

 Gymnasts and high divers often do some remarkable spinning between the diving board and the pool. How do they do that without being able to push off of something? When a diver's feet leave the board, she has all the angular momentum she's going to get. If she's somersaulting (spinning around her transverse axis) she can change the speed of her spin by tucking or extending her body. (See "Taking a Dive" on page 46.) You can see this clearly in a gymnast on the uneven parallel bars. She may start out doing a giant swing around that upper bar. When she lets go of the bar and tucks her body, however, she decreases the distance between much of her mass and the axis around which she's rotating. So she starts spinning much faster—sometimes as much as twenty times faster than her rate of spin in the extended position.

You can change the speed of just about any spin by changing the distance between your mass and the axis of rotation. If a diver is twisting around her longitudinal axis, she can speed up the spin by throwing one arm across her chest and the other behind her head. This is called "squaring up."

Taking a Dive

The laws of physics are great equalizers. Take gravity, for example. Step off the roof of a building, and it doesn't matter who you are, you accelerate toward the earth at a screaming rate of 0 to 60 miles per hour in three seconds. Some people manage to make falling from three stories an act of breathtaking grace. Case in point: platform divers.

Starting from a dead standstill on a ledge 33 feet in the air, there's a brief swing of the arms, a leap, and suddenly the diver is whirling in a blur of somersaulting limbs, finally slicing into the water with a muted *floosh* that barely makes a splash. By slowing down the action on Becky Ruehl's back 2½ somersault pike, we were able to spot some of the physics tricks that make falling look good.

1 The takeoff is crucial. As she leaves the board, she needs to be spinning with enough angular momentum to make 2½ somersaults before hitting the water. She'll get this angular momentum using her arms and legs.

2 In preparation, she winds up her arms with a roundhouse swing. Meanwhile, she lets herself fall slightly backwards as she drops into a crouch. The farther out her center of gravity is from the platform, the more leverage her legs will have when she pushes off.

3 With an explosive burst, she flings her arms and torso backward while pushing off with her legs. Together, these two motions set her spinning. She has to get all the angular momentum she needs right now—once her feet leave the board, she can't get any more.

4 With the water less than two seconds away, she'd better hurry up and get in those 2½ somersaults. To do them, she'll use the angular momentum she acquired during her launch.

5 By tucking her body in, she reduces her angular inertia and speeds up her spin. She's not gaining angular momentum this way, she's just adjusting her body to exploit the angular momentum she already has.

6 Now that she's rocketing towards the water at nearly 40 miles an hour, she needs to stop spinning and straighten out. There's no way she can stop herself from spinning altogether, but she can slow down her rotation by getting out of her tuck and extending her body.

7 Fully extended, her angular inertia is so great that her rotation is barely noticeable and she seems to knife straight into the water. Of course, timing is everything: she has to hit the water just as her spinning body is vertical. Otherwise, she'll hit with a splash and the commentators will say rude things about her form.

My Spinning Head

For divers and gymnasts and other spinning athletes, dizziness is a hazard of the trade. You may have noticed that if you spin around in a circle quickly, dizziness doesn't set in until after you stop spinning. The semicircular canals of your inner ear are filled with a fluid called *endolymph*. When you're spinning around in a circle, the endolymph fluid starts sloshing around in the inner ear. This excites tiny hairs, called the *crista*. When you stop spinning, that fluid keeps sloshing, and the crista send signals that you are still moving, even though your body is actually stationary. To avoid that dizziness, a ballerina uses a technique called "spotting"; she chooses one spot across the room, keeps an eye on it as she spins her head away from it, then whips her head around to see it again. By keeping her head generally stable, she keeps the dizziness at bay.

Figure skaters spin too quickly to use the spotting technique. Instead, when a skater stops, she tosses her head in the opposite direction from her spin. This looks kind of defiant or perky. But it actually serves to get the endolymph lined up again. And divers count the number of times they see the sky and the water to figure out when they're supposed to stop spinning.

The Limits

Will humans ever hit the peak of their swiftness, height, and strength? It seems like we are beginning to slow the rate at which we are breaking records. Since 1976, the women's 400-meter freestyle record has dropped only eight seconds, and no one has beaten Janet Evans's 4:03.85 at the 1988 Seoul Olympics. Indeed, only four world swimming records were established at Atlanta in 1996, as compared to eight in Barcelona in 1992. In track and field, between 1968 and 1980, an average of 9.25 track and field world records were established at each Olympics. But from 1984 to 1996, only 2.25 were established—at Atlanta, only two world records were made.

What gives—or doesn't give? There are some physical limits to human performance. One limit is simply our metabolism. The body can only pump out so much blood, consume so much oxygen, convert so much ATP into muscular power. In a 1990 UCLA study, Dr. Jared Diamond found that humans, like 36 other species, generally can't expend more than seven times the amount of energy in motion that they expend at rest. In other words, you can pour it on and pour it on, but at a certain point the bottle is empty.

The body's structure, too, has its limits. Many physiologists believe that humans will never be able to jump much over eight feet in the high jump because the human muscles and bones can't take any more impact than that; they believe the same thing about a 30-foot long jump.

In 1996, Donavan Bailey ran 100 meters in 9.84 seconds. A cheetah could run the same distance in less than half the time. On the other hand, it would take a giant tortoise about 22 minutes to cover the same course.

One area in which we may continue to see improvement, however, is in women's records, simply because women are receiving better training and being given more opportunities. In the last twelve years, the women's record for the marathon dropped more than 23 minutes, while the men's dropped only 22 seconds. And where the men's 400-meter freestyle record has sunk only 1'14" seconds over the last 73 years, the women's has plummeted more than two minutes, overtaking Mark Spitz's 1968 record for men.

Our technology allows us to look at things in the most microscopic detail, from measurements of caloric intake, kicking efficiency, and oxygen consumption to digitized representations of a biker's balance, a runner's stride, and a long jumper's leg position. This analysis allows us to measure and improve tiny aspects of human performance. But in the future, we may not be creating better and better athletes, but better and better clocks and measuring tapes, ones that will reward athletes who win by millionths of a second, or 10 millionths of a meter.

Physicist Party Trick

We asked Exploratorium physicist Thomas Humphrey for an experiment that involved bodies spinning as they fell through the air—and his eyes lit up. "We need a rubber band and a hardcover book that's taller than it is wide," he said. Then he showed us this neat trick.

First, put the rubber band around the book so that the book won't open up when you toss it in the air.

The book can spin in three different ways. It can spin around the median axis, a line drawn through the middle of the book, from front cover to back.

Hold the book by one corner and toss it in the air so that it spins around the median axis. No problem.

The book can also spin around its longitudinal axis, a line that's drawn from the top of the book to the bottom of the book, the long way.

Hold the book by its spine and toss it in the air so that it spins around the longitudinal axis. Once again—no problem.

But the book can also spin around its transverse axis, a line that's drawn across the width of the book, through the middle.

Hold the book by the lower two corners and toss it so that it spins around the transverse axis.

Wow! Try that again! Rather than just spinning, the book spins and simultaneously flips. Weird.

What's going on?

A lot of books and equations got thrown around in our attempts to understand this one. When we told Thomas we wanted him to explain it to us without higher mathematics, he grumbled, but finally came up with the following.

The key is the shape of the book. Take a good hard look at it and you'll notice it has three dimensions, and none of them are the same (i.e., it's taller than it is wide and wider than it is thick). This makes the book either harder or easier to get spinning, depending on which way you spin it. The spin around the median axis is the hardest to get going, the spin around the longitudinal axis is the easiest, and the wacky spin around the transverse axis is somewhere in between.

A more impressive way to talk about this is in terms of moment of inertia. (Thomas does like to impress—after all, he is a physicist.) Moment of inertia is just a measure of how hard it is to get something spinning. So another way to say that the median spin is the hardest to get started is to say that the book has its largest moment of inertia around the median axis. Likewise, the moment of inertia around the longitudinal axis is the smallest, and the moment of inertia around the transverse axis is, again, somewhere in between.

When an object spins around an axis for which the moment of inertia is *not* the smallest or the largest, the spin is unstable. Unstable means that instead of spinning contentedly about the original axis, the book spontaneously starts spinning around the other two axes also. With all three spins happening at once, the book suddenly starts to flip and whirl like an Olympic diver. According to Thomas, this similarity is no accident—what works for the book also works for the human body.

3 Collisions and Abuse

SPORT, WROTE sociologist Thorstein Veblen in 1899, is "an expression of the barbaric temperament." As such, sport involves competition, the will to succeed, and a lot of people smashing into each other, smashing into things, and smashing things into other things.

If you play or watch sports, you probably take most of these collisions for granted. When you run, your feet collide with the ground. When you play tennis, your racket collides with the ball. When you play defensive tackle for a football team, you pretty much sign up for running into large, moving men on a regular basis. But some collisions—or the repetition of many collisions—can result in undesirable consequences. There are minor injuries: cuts, bruises, abrasions, sprains, and twists. There are horrible injuries: broken spines, snapped necks, and bleeding brains that result in paralysis or death. And there's all the stuff in between: broken clavicles, cracked ribs, torn knee ligaments, smashed noses, fractured jaws, pulled muscles, and the like.

In the last two decades, sports medicine has come a long way towards preventing injuries and then speeding athletes' recovery. Protective equipment has come a long way too. But even the fanciest equipment can't keep an athlete from taking a fall. And even the most sophisticated medical techniques and equipment can't guarantee that an injured athlete will be able to return to his or her sport. Collisions are governed by the rules of physics and physiology; sometimes you can't fool around with Mother Nature.

OOPH! The Physics of a Collision

Spectators tend to look at collisions in terms of both pain and achievement. ("Gee, that must have hurt! But, uh, how many yards did he gain?") When physicists wear their physicists' hats, they look at collisions very differently. (When they wear the home team cap, of course, they're rooting just like the rest of us.)

Football is particularly susceptible to analysis by physicists. There are so many questions a physicist could answer. What really happens when two football players run into each other on the field? How much force is involved? How much energy? Could we use that energy to lift a car? To light up all the lights in the stadium?

Suppose you want to figure out the energy involved in a collision between two football players. According to the physicists, the only things that matter to this calculation are how fast the players are moving and how much mass each player has.

Ordinary people often talk about weight and mass as if they were the same thing, but physicists are careful to distinguish between the two. Exploratorium physicist Paul Doherty explained why. "In outer space, objects are weightless—but they still have mass." In space, you can tell how massive a weightless object is by noting how big a push it takes to get the thing moving and how big a push it takes to stop it once it's moving. But here on earth, a football player's weight is closely related to his mass. Physicists get very picky when talking about weight and mass, but if you aren't a physicist, you can just think of "weight" when we say "mass," and you'll be on the right track.

If you know a player's mass and speed, you can figure out his kinetic energy, which is the energy of motion. The kinetic energy of a moving football player is just half the guy's mass *(m)* multiplied by his speed squared. Or, as Exploratorium physicist Thomas Humphrey scrawled it on a pad: Energy = $\frac{1}{2}mv^2$.

Energy can't be created or destroyed. All you can do is change it from one form to another. (Remember that from your high school science classes? As Thomas says, "It's fun to remember your physics! I'm always very happy to remember mine.") Now you know how to figure out the players' kinetic energy before they collide. Since they aren't moving after they collide, you know that their kinetic energy is close to zero at that point. So you can figure out how much energy got converted to another form.

When two football players collide, their energy of motion has to go somewhere. That energy goes into deformation, a nice word for getting mashed.

Take a look at the box on page 57 if you want to see all the calculations, but the bottom line is this: the energy of a collision between two football players is enough to lift 23 tons about an inch. Or, if you think in terms of automobiles, this energy could lift a compact car about two feet in the air.

Why should any of this math matter to the players on the field? Remember—that energy has to go somewhere. Where does it go? "When two objects hit, they both deform mightily," Thomas says. "They also rub against each other, which dissipates energy, which turns into heat."

So that energy goes into deformation, a nice word for getting mashed. It can also go into breaking bones. The injuries a player sustains in a collision on the football field depends on two things—the mass and speed of the guy who hits him. You probably knew that already—but now you know exactly how much it matters.

The same equation applies to any other sport that involves collision—where bats collide with balls, where feet collide with pavement, where fists collide with faces. To calculate the energy, you need to know how much the moving thing weighs and how fast it's moving. You can punch harder if you put more weight behind the punch or if you move your fist faster.

Colleen Rosensteel, the 210-pound U.S. Olympic judo heavyweight, asked how she felt about possibly facing 300-pound opponents, said, "It's not so much trouble throwing them—it's watching that you don't land underneath them."

There are other ways to look at the collision between the two football players. Paul Doherty shared one approach with us. In a collision like this, one person almost always ends up on his butt. That person isn't necessarily the smaller guy, although that's part of it. And it's not necessarily the guy with the least speed, although that's part of it too. Instead, the guy on his butt is the guy who has the least linear momentum, which is the mass multiplied by the velocity. If the smaller guy is going fast enough, he'll actually have more linear momentum than the big guy who's standing still or just jogging along.

If you want to change the momentum of something or someone, Paul says, you have to apply a force. How much force you have to apply depends on how much momentum the moving thing has. It's hard to stop a drifting ocean liner (lots of mass; low velocity) and it's hard to stop a 45-caliber bullet (small mass; high velocity).

So suppose there's a big lineman coming at you at full speed and you want to stop him, reducing his momentum to zero. How do you do it? You can say, "hey look man, I'm just a fan," which only works if you're not wearing a uniform. Another method would be to apply a force to change his momentum. You could apply a small force over a long time (grabbing onto his jersey as he runs past and dragging along

Wham! Bam! Boom! with Math

On third down and ten, Dallas Cowboys running back Emmitt Smith takes the hand-off and heads upfield. He's stopped cold, just short of the first-down yardage, when he runs head-on into sprinting San Francisco 49ers linebacker Gary Plummer. The sound of crashing helmets and bodies resounds throughout the stadium. Exactly how much energy is involved in this collision?

To answer that question, we need to know each man's mass (m) and how fast he's moving at the time of the collision (his velocity, v). From player rosters, we know Plummer weighs 247 pounds, Smith 209. To satisfy the physicists, we need to convert their weights in pounds into masses in kilograms. There are 2.2 pounds in a kilogram, so Plummer's mass is 112 kilograms, and Smith's is 95.

It's not unusual for a running back like Smith to cover 8 yards in a second. This corresponds (in metric units) to about 7.3 meters/second. For this play, Plummer's speed is slower, a more sedate 6.2 meters/sec (or a little under 7 yards a second).

As he runs, each player has energy because of his motion (what physicists call his kinetic energy) equal to $\frac{1}{2}mv^2$. Because both players are stopped by the collision, the total energy involved is the sum of each man's individual kinetic energy. The unit physicists use for energy is called a joule. Here are the calculations:

Energy (Smith) = $\frac{1}{2}$ x 95 kilograms x (7.3 meters/sec)^2
= 2531 joules

Energy (Plummer) = $\frac{1}{2}$ x 112 kilograms x (6.2 meters/sec)^2
= 2153 joules

The total energy involved in the collision is therefore:
2531 + 2153 = 4684 joules.

How much energy is that? Well, it's enough to move a 23-ton object one inch!

If we know how long the collision lasted, we can also convert the collision's energy to power. The unit of power we're most familiar with is the watt (as in a 100-watt light bulb). A watt is defined as the amount of power that will provide one joule of energy for one second. To convert our collision energy to power, we need to divide the energy by the time of the collision—in this case, about .3 seconds. The power generated in this collision is therefore: 4684/(.3) = 14052 watts or roughly 14 kilowatts. During the .3 second of the collision, that energy could power 140 100-watt light bulbs.

The energy of a collision between two football players is enough to lift 23 tons about an inch— or to lift a compact car about two feet into the air. (See page 56 for the calculations.)

behind until he slows to a stop or turns around and comes back to kill you). Or if you are the appropriate size, you could apply a large force over a short time, running head-on into him.

You have the choice because of something physicists call impulse. Impulse is simply your force multiplied by the length of time that you apply it. Time matters because the longer your collision takes, the less force you need, relatively speaking. Jumping out a window onto a pile of mattresses is easier on your body than jumping out a window onto concrete. That's because the pile of mattresses applies a force to slow you down gradually and the concrete stops you abruptly. Since impulse is equal to the time multiplied by the force, the longer the time, the less force you need. You have the same stopping impulse in both cases and you get the same result—but the force on your body is very different. If you are about to collide with something, anything you can do to increase the time over which the collision takes place will minimize the force on your body.

OW! The Physics of an Injury

Of course, 300-pound linemen, 200-pound hockey players, and even 160-pound baseball players don't just collide, fall down, and then skip or skate away. Instead, even the simplest collision can wreak havoc in your body. As Thomas mentioned, collisions often deform an object. And in sports the object deformed is often the human body.

When a foreign object hits your body, it impacts a number of different structures. It can compress and activate nerve endings. (A fist in the eyeball activates retinal neurons, for instance; that's why we see "stars.") It can break the skin, and rupture the veins beneath it, causing bleeding. It can rupture the veins and damage the tissue without breaking the skin. (That's what's known as a bruise, or a hematoma.) Any tissue damage results in inflammation, one of your body's defense mechanisms. When an area is inflamed, more blood flows to the injured tissue, bringing in *phagocytes,* cells that engulf and destroy invading bacteria and other foreign material, and prepare for repair of the damaged tissue. A collision can also stretch or tear tendons, ligaments, or muscles; it can twist, unhinge, or otherwise misalign a joint. Joints are among the most fragile structures in the human body.

Any impact that causes (or comes close to causing) tissue damage usually also causes pain. As you may have noticed, different people respond to pain in different ways. According to Dr. David Janda, an orthopedic surgeon at the Institute for Preventative Sports Medicine, some of this difference may be physiological—but a lot is psychological. Dr. Janda says, "There are pain fibers and it seems that some people have more pain fibers or more hyper-reactive pain than others. But pain also has a psychological component. Some people come into my office and they say, 'hey you know this isn't so bad.' Others come in with the same injury and they're writhing and screaming. Some of it is attitude. Some of it is what we call 'secondary gain,' or people who get something else out of their pain, like attention. And some people panic when they have pain, which makes the pain seem even worse."

One other thing that affects how much damage (and pain) a collision can cause is pressure. Pressure is simply force per unit of area. A large force, distributed over a large area, will do less damage than the same force concentrated in a small area.

Why is a karate strike like a woman in high heels on a golf course? In both cases, force is concentrated on a small area. The spikes of the high heels sink into the turf because much of the woman's weight is pushing on that small point. If she were wearing her running shoes (which we hope she'd rather be), that same weight would be spread over the broad surface of the heel and she wouldn't sink into the grass. By striking with the edge of the hand, the knuckles, the edge of the foot, or the heel, a karate black belt focuses the force of the strike on a small area in order to do maximum damage at the point of contact.

Protective padding for sports is designed to spread the force of a point of impact over a wide area, thereby lessening the force on any one point. Boxing gloves, for instance, spread out the force of the striking fist, rather than focusing all of that force on one small area. By spreading out the force, gloves make it easier for a boxer to hit hard without damaging his own fragile hand bones. That means that a boxer can hit his opponent much harder without injuring himself. This, in turn, helps determine the type of injuries sustained in a fight. If you are wearing boxing gloves when you hit someone, the force of the blow is distributed across the front of the glove, which will mostly cause your *opponent's* head to snap back. (A good punch to the head can cause the head to accelerate backwards at about 80 times the acceleration of gravity.)

Since a boxer wearing gloves is less likely to injure himself, he can hit his opponent harder. In fact, some people have advocated returning to bare-knuckle boxing in an attempt to lessen the violence and injuries associated with the sport. Abandoning the use of gloves would result in more broken hands, but fewer broken heads.

Collisions affect different parts of the body in different ways and with differing levels of severity. We're going to examine some of these collisions and their consequences, starting from the ground up.

How does ice help a sprained ankle or other injury?

Cold helps cut down on swelling by shrinking the blood vessels. This reduces bleeding and therefore swelling in the affected area. Cold also helps keep the muscles from spasming (contracting uncontrollably) and relieves pain.

But too much cold can damage the skin, which is why you should apply ice for a while, take a break, then apply it again. This allows the skin to return to normal temperature between treatments.

Generally speaking, you should apply ice for 10 to 30 minutes, depending on the body part and your own comfort level. Areas with little body fat (like the ankle, knee, and elbow) cannot handle cold as well as fatty areas (like the thigh and buttocks). A bag of frozen peas can make an excellent substitute for an ice bag, since the peas will better mold to the shape of your ankle (or knee or whatever).

Cold gel packs that can be frozen and refrozen cool the skin faster than an ordinary ice bag and should only be applied for short periods. Chemical cold bags (which stay at room temperature until squeezing mixes the chemicals inside) don't get as cold as an icebag, and can stay on the skin for longer periods of time.

Cold therapy may not be recommended for people who are very sensitive to cold, those with blood vessels too near the skin, and diabetics and others who have problems with diminished blood flow. If you're one of those people, you should talk to your doctor about applying ice to an injury.

Heat can also relax muscles and relieve pain, but it makes swelling worse by stimulating blood flow. That's why cold is best immediately following an injury and for at least 48 hours afterward, or until the swelling goes down. Then heat can help, as the increased blood flow "cleans" out the damaged area.

My Aching Feet

Probably no part of the human body takes as much consistent pounding as the human foot. Its 26 bones, 33 joints, and more than 100 muscles, tendons, and ligaments fire sprints, launch leaps, and absorb the shocks of stops, starts, twists, turns, and landings. (Your two feet's 500,000 sweat glands help keep those active little levers cool.) In fact, in just three miles of running, a 150-pound man's feet strike the ground about 5000 times (for about a quarter of a second at a time). With each step, that man lands with a force that can be up to three times his body weight at foot contact. His body has to absorb the repeated jarring of that force. Even if you aren't a runner, your feet probably work pretty hard. Most people take an average of 9000 steps in the course of a day.

"These are my new shoes. They're good shoes. They won't make you rich like me, they won't make you rebound like me, they definitely won't make you handsome like me. They'll only make you have shoes like me. That's it."

—Charles Barkley of the Houston Rockets, in a commercial for basketball shoes

With every step you take, your foot needs to be springy, to absorb the shock of the collision with the ground. But it also needs to be stiff, so that it can push off from the ground. To accomplish both goals, your foot bones form three arches: the familiar, tall one that runs along the inner edge of your foot; a flatter arch along the outer edge; and a third arch that goes from one side of the sole to the other.

When you take a step, these arches flatten and store energy. When your foot lifts off again, the arches release this energy, putting a spring in your step. At the moment that you lift your foot, your springy foot also *supinates*—that is, it rolls outwards, away from the main arch. This rolling motion changes the arrangement of your foot bones so that they lock together to make the stiff lever you need to push off the ground. As you step and the foot lands again, it *pronates*. That is, it rolls inwards at the arch. At the same time, it becomes flexible and springy again.

Why should you care about how your foot tilts as you run? Well, what happens at ground level affects the rest of your body; your feet are the foundation of posture and performance. "Even the position of the big toe can affect lower leg dynamics," notes Dr. Jeffrey Ross, president of the American Association of Podiatric Sports Medicine. "This in turn affects the knees, pelvis, lower back, and neck." Foot positions can also affect swings, jumps, and the amount of power an athlete can generate while running or cycling. In other words, the foot bone's connected to every other bone, so it needs to be healthy.

Different sports pose different risks to the feet. In general, lateral movement, strong impact, and bursts of speed or power cause the most damage. Worst case scenario? Basketball players who routinely slide, rock, or hop from side to side during defense and then spring up and down during offense, periodically landing on the uneven terrain of other people's feet.

Though almost every athlete is vulnerable to foot injuries, most of these problems result from over-exertion or inadequate training, which means they can be prevented. Some of the most common injuries of the foot and the leg start with the tilt of the foot.

If your feet roll too far inward with each step, you have excessive pronation. With each step, excessive pronation can cause excessive stress elsewhere in the body. If you're a runner, excessive pronation may result in or contribute to common sports ailments such as runner's knee, lower leg pain or "shin splints," heel pain from the plantar fascia (a long flat tissue that lies between the heel and the ball of the foot), and inflammation of the Achilles tendon. People who have excessive pronation also tend to have low arches; their footprint tends to show the entire foot.

People with high arches are likely to have the opposite problem. Their foot doesn't pronate enough, which means it's not as good a shock absorber as it should be. Both excessive pronation and too little pronation can be corrected with orthotics, foam wedges built to compensate for foot faults and inserted into shoes to change the positioning and motion of your feet as you run.

In general, your shoes are an important factor in preventing injuries resulting from foot problems. Feet provide the first line of shock absorption as we run and walk (the muscles and joints in the rest of the body absorb the rest). Shoes that are cushioned help slow down the collision time, resulting in less shock hitting the body. Unfortunately, the foam that most shoes use for cushioning breaks down after about 60 miles or so. The search for the perfect substitute has inspired some designers to inject all sorts of weird stuff into shoe soles, including inert gases, bags of silicon fluid, even a lining that can be inflated with a little pump on the shoe tongue.

"If horses won't eat it, I don't want to play on it."

—Dick Allen of the Philadelphia Phillies, on AstroTurf

You may have wondered if it really matters whether you wear a shoe designed for a specific sport. According to podiatrists, it can. If you play tennis, racquetball, and other sports requiring much side-to-side motion, you're better off with a shoe that provides lateral stability. If your shoe doesn't provide this stability, you run a greater risk of an ankle sprain. If you're a runner, you're usually moving in a straight line and lateral stability isn't as important. Running shoes usually have several features that shoes designed for tennis lack: heel elevation to reduce stress on the Achilles tendon, more shock absorption, and better pronation control.

Another thing that affects your feet is the surface you run or play on. The springiness of the surface influences how much shock your body will have to absorb with each step. New and improved track surfaces have increased springiness to help reduce injuries to sprinters. (See Chapter 2, page 30.) The friction between your shoe and the surface also affects how quickly you can stop, twist, and turn—and that, in turn, affects your feet and knees.

That Nasty Turf

AstroTurf is a playing surface that has become notorious for some of the problems it has created. AstroTurf looks like grass, but it's actually nylon fibers stitched into a mat, laid over a foam pad, and then glued to an asphalt base. An AstroTurf-covered field is harder than a grassy one, and it gets even harder as it ages, contributing to soreness, shin splints, and tendonitis. On AstroTurf, players can't dig in with their big toes to get a push off as they run. If the foot slips, the big toe may hyperextend. That sprains the ligaments that support the toe, an ailment known as turf toe.

Most worrisome, though, are the spate of gruesome knee injuries sustained on AstroTurf, attributable, primarily, to the extraordinary traction provided. Traction usually seems like a

The Origin of AstroTurf

AstroTurf came about when Roy Hofheinz ("The Judge") decided in 1965 that he wanted to build the world's first climate-controlled coliseum for his baseball team, the Houston Astros. When the Astrodome opened a year later, it was the largest air-conditioned space of any kind in the world. There was just one problem: the skylights in the roof created such glare during day games that the outfielders couldn't see the ball. The club covered the panels with dark paint, which caused the grass on the field to die. They tried painting the dead grass green, but that didn't work either. So Hofheinz contacted Monsanto, which was developing artificial grass for inner city kids to play on, and arranged to have some of that artificial grass installed in the Astrodome. Within a decade, most indoor coliseums had followed suit. Within two decades, a number of outdoor stadiums had followed suit as well.

good thing. But if the feet get stuck in one place while your body tries to twist or lunge to another place, something has to give. Too often it's the knee.

You might think knee injuries would occur most often during tackling, but some pretty nasty injuries have happened when no one else is even near. In 1993, for instance, Chicago Bears wide receiver Wendell Davis severed both of his patellar tendons when he planted his feet to jump for a pass on the AstroTurf at Philadelphia's Veteran Stadium. That very same day, some 1000 miles to the west at the Hoosier Dome, Indianapolis Colts defensive tackle Steve Emtman ripped his anterior cruciate ligament, his medial collateral ligament, and his patellar tendon when he turned to tackle Dallas's Emmet Smith. Neither Davis nor Emtman had collided with someone else—they just made a bad turn on a bad surface.

What's the answer? Most new stadiums are putting old-fashioned grass back on the field now. Other stadiums are experimenting with newfangled turf products that combine real grass with synthetics and woven mats to provide the "playability of grass and the durability of AstroTurf," says Clark Gaines, regional director of the National Football League Players Association. "The trend is definitely away from AstroTurf now."

My Twinging Knee and Other Leg Laments

If feet take the most pressure in sports, knees take the most abuse. Seventy-five percent of all serious sports injuries have to do with this joint, which connects the thighbone (femur) and the shinbone (tibia), via wedges of cartilage.

Lunge to the left or right too quickly, or suddenly stop your down-court sprint, and you can tear the cartilage, which doesn't repair too well on its own. (Doctors usually recommend removing it, which can lead to chronic soreness during competitions and arthritis in later years, but that does allow athletes to compete.)

Another common problem is *chondromalacia* (also called "runner's knee"), a painful condition caused by uneven wear on the cartilage under the kneecap. A variety of factors contribute to chondromalacia, including weak quadriceps and lack of balance among muscles, hill running, overtraining, and over- or under-pronating feet. In bad cases you can actually feel and hear that grinding when the knee is flexed. Sports docs suggest that strengthening the quadriceps will help correct and prevent this problem.

Injuries to knee ligaments are a more serious problem. The ligaments are responsible for holding the different pieces of the knee together, but ligaments aren't very stretchy, so they can break. Both the anterior cruciate ligament (ACL) and the side ligaments of the knee are torn more often than the other five ligaments in the knee. The ACL, in fact, is stretched or torn in more than half of all knee injuries. It's a bad one to damage because its poor blood supply means it rarely heals even if it's sewn back together.

A few years ago, a number of researchers discovered that women athletes (in cross-country running, basketball, soccer, skiing, and volleyball) were suffering more ACL tears than male athletes. (In basketball, according to one study, the ratio was as much as 6 to 1.) Researchers aren't sure why this happens. It could be due to differences in anatomy (women tend to have less-developed thigh muscles, narrower pelvises, and wider femoral notches, through which the ACL runs). Or it could be due to differences in early training. Girls traditionally aren't as active in early years, which means that their tendons and ligaments don't develop as well.

As with feet problems, knee problems are more often than not a result of overtraining—running too many days consecutively, doing too much

My Twisted Knee

It seems as if at least once during every football game you watch on TV, a player has to be helped off the field because of a knee injury. Football players and other athletes often put extreme forces on their knees, for example, by making a sudden cut to avoid being tackled. When the knee is stressed beyond what it can handle, something inside has to give. And that something is often one of the ligaments that hold the knee together.

There are seven ligaments in the knee. These bands of strong, somewhat flexible tissue connect the leg bones and limit their motions. The ligaments stretch a little (about six percent of their length), but, if pushed farther, they can break or tear. One ligament in particular is involved in most of the serious knee injuries—the anterior cruciate ligament, or ACL, which runs from the front of the shinbone to the back of the thighbone (it is one of two ligaments that crisscross through the center of the knee joint). The ACL helps stabilize the knee by limiting its rotation as well as the forward motion of the thighbone.

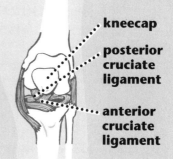

kneecap

posterior cruciate ligament

anterior cruciate ligament

But if you twist your knee too much when it's bent and then straightened, as when a running back suddenly stops and cuts to the side, the ACL can stretch too much and tear, sometimes with an audible crack or pop. Normally a partially torn ligament will, given time and rest, repair itself. However, having been stretched, the ligament never returns to its original shape. As a result, your knee may become chronically unstable, "giving out" when you try to make a sharp turn to the right or left.

If the ACL doesn't heal (and due to its poor blood supply, it usually doesn't mend well), or if it's completely torn, a surgeon may have to sew it back together again. Even then, it may not heal all the way, in which case, it may have to be replaced. During reconstruction, a new ACL is created from small pieces of the patellar tendon (which connects the kneecap to the thighbone) or from tendons in the back of the thigh. These are then threaded through small tunnels cut in the thigh- and shin-bones themselves and secured.

Strengthening your leg muscles, especially the hamstring in the back of your leg, will help stabilize your knee after an injury. And many doctors recommend you wear a hinged knee brace to protect the joint. Can you come back to your sport after a serious knee injury? Yes, but it's not easy, and only you can decide if it's worth all the pain and work necessary.

distance too fast on the bicycle, or grinding up and down hills when the cartilage is already suffering. Strengthening the quadriceps and hamstrings can help keep the knee in place. Stretching religiously can keep muscles around the knee flexible enough to absorb sudden stops and starts. And wearing shoes that slip a bit can help prevent the jam-on-the-brakes kind of stops that send athletes crumpling to the floor.

Sports medicine advances like arthroscopy and endoscopy have been crucial for repairing knee injuries without causing more problems. So too have advances in physical therapy. When Ki-Jana Carter, a rookie with the Cincinnati Bengals and the NFL's top draft pick in 1995, tore his ACL that same year, he was able to come back after one season, instead of the normal two, primarily because of his extraordinary rehab efforts. The Bengals hired an assistant trainer to primarily work on Carter's knee and invested in stationary bikes, stairclimbers, and other equipment. Ten months later Carter was practicing on the field, and he was back in the game for the 1996 season.

Pain in the Neck/Pain in the Back

The back and neck are vulnerable to injury because they house the spinal cord, which is basically the information highway of the human body. In fact, the spinal cord is an extension of the brain itself. The brain sends impulses out to the body via the spinal cord and the body sends impulses back to the brain via the same route. These impulses include both conscious movements ("I think I'll eat some of those grapes.") and unconscious movements (making sure organs and blood vessels do their job properly).

"No more than usual."

—Boston Red Sox first baseman Dick Stuart (aka Dr. Strangeglove) when asked if he felt dizzy after being hit by a pitch

The spinal cord consists of a long bundle of nerve fibers that extends from just above the small of your back to the base of your brain. Vertebrae, or rings of bone, encase the cord. If those vertebrae get jarred, fractured, or broken, they can actually sever the spinal cord, thus blocking impulses from the brain to the limbs.

In football, shoulder pads and neck rolls are designed to keep the neck from moving too much. Still, there have been a number of high-profile neck and back injuries in sports. (In fact, sports accidents only account for 7 percent of all spinal cord injuries, but media coverage makes it seem like there are more.) Football players Dennis Byrd, Darryl Stingley, and Mike Utley; actor and equestrian Christopher Reeve; and gymnast Julissa Gomez all suffered severe injuries while engaging in sports.

Byrd was lucky: his spinal cord wasn't severed and he received methylprednisone, a steroid that reduces swelling in the spinal cord and so can reduce nerve damage and the extent of the paralysis. He was also one of the very first people to receive GM1, an experimental drug that suppresses a hormone that releases amino acids in the spinal cord upon injury. Those amino acids can actually eat away at tissue in the spinal cord.

Byrd can now walk, and spinal specialists are looking to both methylprednisone and GM1 as keys to helping other people with injured spinal cords. But Utley, Stingley, and Reeve all remain at least partially paralyzed. Julissa Gomez died after breaking her neck during a vault in Tokyo.

Of course, there are other, less severe injuries that occur to the spinal column. Many athletes suffer from something called "stingers," or "burners," which are nerve injuries that occur after an athlete gets hit (or falls) on her head, neck, or shoulder. True to their name, these nerve injuries often manifest as a burning or stinging sensation in the neck or arm, or as numbness or tingling. These sometimes go away on their own; more often they require rehabilitation exercises to thoroughly heal the nerves. Prevention involves building up the crucial muscles behind the shoulder and along the upper back and wearing properly fitted protective equipment.

Bruising the Brain

Injuries to the head are perhaps the most frightening since these can result in instant death. The brain is protected by the skull, and head injuries usually have to do with the brain smacking up against the inside of the skull and sustaining damage that way.

Since 1900, surgeons have been examining the brains of boxers for information about head injuries. They've found that different hits produce different injuries. If your head rotates to either side, the cranial vein or long nerve fibers inside the skull can stretch or tear, resulting in a bruise or nerve damage. If the vein ruptures, the leaking blood "compresses the brain, which can cause death minutes, hours, or days later," says George Lundberg, editor of the *Journal of the American Medical Association*. (That's what happened to Duk Koo Kim in 1982,

when Ray "Boom-Boom" Mancini hit him in the head.) The leaking blood can also clot, as happened with Michael Watson in 1991 and Gerald McClellan in 1995. Watson is now paralyzed. McClellan is "pretty much out of it," Lundberg says.

A blow to the head can do considerable damage—even if it doesn't kill you. A bruise on the cerebral cortex can seriously impair your God-given rights to see straight, remember who you are, consider a new career path, or take out your own mouth guard. A blow to the head can damage the cerebellum (which governs balance and muscle movement and receives signals from the skin and muscles) or the brain stem, which coordinates muscle movement and consciousness, respiration, and heart function. A blow to the neck can injure the carotid artery, one of the major arteries in the brain.

Feeling a little queasy? That's just a one-time punch. Chronic brain injury leads to, well, chronic brain damage. Some boxers, most notably Mohammad Ali, have developed symptoms similar to those of Parkinson's disease. Others develop cognitive and personality changes that physicians call "dementia pugilistica" and "chronic progressive traumatic encephalopathy of

"It doesn't matter if you're a famous boxer or just someone who's used as a sparring partner— which is the equivalent of being a punching bag in my mind. The damage still occurs."

—George Lundberg, editor of the Journal of the American Medical Association

boxers." Lay people call it being "punch drunk" and it's a very real syndrome, marked first by emotional disturbances and mild lack of coordination, then paranoia and tremors, and finally a decrease in general cognitive functions, memory and hearing loss, more loss of coordination, and aggressiveness and suspicion. Somewhere between 10 and 25 percent of all professional boxers end up truly punch drunk. "You have to understand that each blow creates a little tearing, a little cell loss, even if there's no concussion," notes Lundberg. "It doesn't matter if you're a famous boxer or just someone who's used as a sparring partner—which is the equivalent of being a punching bag in my mind. The damage still occurs."

Head injuries are just serious enough that some organizations, including the American Medical Association, advocate banning boxing. But many believe that completely banning something as popular and lucrative as boxing would simply send it underground, where the lack of regulation could result in even worse injuries. Instead, most matches now have ringside surgeons and ambulances waiting.

Changes in equipment have also been advocated, including using helmets. These would protect against bruises (by distributing the force of impact), but wouldn't prevent the head from whipping back and forth.

By way of comparison, the use of helmets in football have helped prevent some facial injuries and skull cracks, but have given rise to other kinds of injuries. Stronger helmets have encouraged players to use their heads as battering rams, which has resulted in spinal cord injuries, broken necks, and concussions for the offensive players. Rougher play and harder fields are also resulting in more concussions for those being tackled; New York Jets wide receiver Al Toon retired in 1992 because he had suffered nine concussions in eight years.

Modern helmet designs include both the RushAir SpineSaver, which is essentially an airbag inside a football helmet (it inflates if a sensor detects 500 pounds of force) and the ProCap, a polyurethane shell that attaches to the top part of the helmet. In laboratory tests the ProCap has reduced G-forces transmitted to the skull by an average of 30 percent. Buffalo Bills safety Mark Kelso began wearing it in 1990 after a string of concussions. San Francisco 49ers offensive tackle Steve Wallace has also used it, as have more than 2000 youth, high school, and college players across the country.

If the drama of sports often leads to injuries, the injuries themselves often add drama to the sport. It's not just the heartbreak of seeing a great athlete felled on the field. It's also the drama of seeing a great athlete overcome an injury and return to the field. Wayne Gretzky developed a herniated thoracic disk (caused, most likely, by getting whammed from behind during fourteen seasons on the ice), but he returned to the hockey rink to play in the World Cup in 1996 and then joined the New York Rangers. Buddy Lazier, who won the Indy 500 in 1996, drove with 16 fractures and 25 chips in his lower backbone and tailbone from a crash three months earlier. During the race, he was traveling at 230 mph—even though he, and everyone else, knew that an accident at that speed could re-shatter his backbone, and possibly kill him. And few were able to watch Muhammad Ali light the 1996 Olympic torch—that beacon of athletic endeavor and performance—without being tremendously moved. Ali was one of the most brilliant boxers of all time, yet spectators held their breath for fear his shaking would cause him to drop the torch. He didn't.

> "The punishment—to the body, the brain, the spirit—a man must endure to become even a moderately good boxer is inconceivable to most of us whose idea of personal risk is largely ego-related or emotional."
> —Joyce Carol Oates, On Boxing

Ouch!

Every sport offers unique opportunities to injure yourself. Here are a few common ailments.

Footballer's Migraine

Repeated, unexpected blows to the head from a soccer ball can initiate migraine headaches.

Shoulder Injuries

Baseball pitchers, skiers, equestrians, and body-surfers are prone to injuries to the rotator cuff, the tendons that attach the shoulder muscles to the bone.

Broken Fingers

In baseball, catchers injure their fingers so frequently that many have trouble wearing World Series rings.

Ankle and Leg Fractures

When skiers wore low boots, ankle fractures were a common injury. With today's higher, rigid boots, a skier is more likely to fracture the tibia and fibula, the two bones that connect the knee and ankle.

Scrum Ear or Wrestler's Ear

A blow can cause bleeding between the ear cartilage and the skin. If the blood is not removed, the ear scars and becomes a cauliflower ear.

Tennis Elbow

This injury can result from overuse of the muscles and tendons used to hit a backhand shot in tennis, or from other repetitive activities that involve bending the wrist backward.

Runner's Knee

Seventy-five percent of all serious sports injuries involve this joint. Ailments range from runner's knee to torn ligaments.

Turf Toe

AstroTurf has been blamed for turf toe, hyperextension of the big toe that happens when an athlete's foot slips on the artificial playing surface.

4 You Gotta Have Balls (and other projectiles)

THE 1886 PECK & Snyder Price List of Out & Indoor Sports & Pastimes offered all sorts of odd-looking athletic equipment, including catcher's mitts that were merely fingerless gloves; "patent solar cork hats" for wear during "the heated term"; and linen jock straps engineered with hooks, laces, and eyelets. But one of the oddest objects is the New Seamless League Ball, which the company advertised as "the best wearing Ball that has ever been offered; the stitch being a blind one, the seam is not exposed to wear, and there is nothing to injure the hands of the player."

Had that ball been adopted, it might very well have spared the delicate hands of baseball players for years to come—although a real mitt would have done a better job. But the game of baseball itself would have become something altogether different. The 108 red cotton double stitches that circumnavigate the modern baseball are vital for a baseball's flight—stitches help keep the ball aloft and determine its path. Without stitches, batters couldn't bat as far, pitchers couldn't pitch as fast, curveballs wouldn't curve as much, and some pitches, like knuckleballs, wouldn't exist at all.

The baseball is just one example of a sports projectile—anything that's thrown or whacked or shot or otherwise motivated to fly through the air. Projectiles are the focus of dozens of sports, which means that athletes and spectators spend a lot of time keeping their eyes on arrows, balls, and platter-shaped things hurtling through the air.

Over the years, sports equipment designers have spent a lot of time tinkering with the shape, weight, and materials of these flying things. And every time they change the projectile, the very nature of the game itself changes. Sometimes it's a little change—the difference between keeping your fielders in close and playing them farther back. Other times it's a big change—the kind that makes officials bellow for new rules or bystanders scurry for cover.

No Stiches Is a Drag

Let's start with a fantasy scenario. Imagine that major league baseball had adopted the Peck & Snyder seamless ball. Smooth balls fly entirely differently than rough balls. When a smooth ball flies, air molecules flow around it to the back, where they meet, mingle, and help push the ball forward. There aren't as many molecules in back as in front, because "shear forces" (that's the effect of oncoming air, not a hairdresser gone mad) rip the calm boundary layer of air from the surface of the ball. This creates a pocket of swirling currents at the back of the

"If I dance after a home run, I don't think the pitchers would appreciate it. Baseball is a different game. In football, you're free to make a fool of yourself."
—Deion Sanders of the Dallas Cowboys and the Cincinnati Reds

ball, like the wake behind a speedboat. Because of those swirling currents, the air pressure right behind the ball is lower than the air pressure in front of the ball. That difference in pressure, a force known as form drag, slows the ball down.

To imagine this form drag from the ball's point of view, think about the last time you had to push your way through a crowd. There were lots of people in front of you (high-pressure air) and there was a bit of a gap behind you, where people hadn't filled in the space you opened (low-pressure air). It took an effort to keep moving forward; it would have been easier to just slide back into the empty space. You were experiencing form drag, just like the smooth ball flying through the air.

Now suppose you added 108 stitches to that smooth ball. When you make a ball's surface rough—by adding stitches (like the ones on a baseball), dimples (like the ones on a golf ball), or fuzz (like the fuzz on a tennis ball), a strange thing happens to the air flowing around the ball. When air flows over a rough surface, the layers of air right next to the ball don't flow as smoothly—they mix and create turbulence, which slows the air flowing past the surface down a little, a effect called surface drag. Rowing shells are so smooth and swimmers shave away speed-stealing hair to try to minimize this surface drag.

A rough surface experiences more surface drag—so you might think that roughening the surface would make a ball move through the air more slowly. Not so! That little bit of turbulence at the surface of the ball helps the air stay by the rough surface longer before it breaks away from the surface and makes a wake of swirling turbulence behind the ball. The longer the air sticks by the surface, the smaller the wake behind the ball. The smaller the wake, the less form drag there is on the ball. With less drag, the ball stays aloft longer and flies faster.

Since the New Seamless League Ball had no stitches, it would be subject to more drag. As a result, it wouldn't fly as fast or as far as a stitched ball. Batters wouldn't be able to hit the seamless ball 475 feet into the outfield and pitchers couldn't pitch balls 80, 90, or 100 miles per hour as they do today.

Ball Speeds

Speed Comparisons

Except for engine-powered machines, balls are the fastest-moving objects in sports. Here are a few speeds, in miles per hour:

Jai alai pelota	188
Golf ball (leaving tee)	170
Tennis ball (after serve)	138
Hockey puck (slapshot)	118
Ping-Pong ball	105
Baseball (fastball)	103
Football	85
Softball	78
Frisbee	74
Bowling ball	15

Compare the ball speeds above to the speed of a:

Downhill skier	65
Cheetah running	63
Horse running	43
Greyhound running	42
Boxing punch	35
Speed skater	31
Sprinter	27
Swimmer	5

Air Is a Real Drag

Moving Slowly

Suppose you've got a smooth ball moving slowly through the air, maybe at about the speed of a softball in a game of slow pitch. The air moving around the ball would look a lot like this. The air flows smoothly, separating in front of the 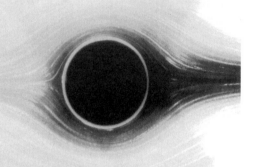 ball and coming back together behind the ball. When the air closes up behind the ball, it helps squirt the ball forward, like a watermelon seed squeezed between your fingers.

Moving Faster

When the same smooth ball moves a little faster, the air doesn't flow all the way around to the back of the ball. Instead, it breaks away from the surface and forms a pocket of swirling currents at the back of the  ball, like the wake behind a speedboat.

Moving Even Faster

When the ball moves even faster, the air breaks away from the surface of the ball even sooner, and the wake behind the ball increases. There's a bigger difference between the pressure in front of the ball and the pressure behind it, and 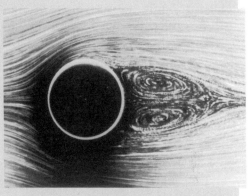 the ball experiences even more drag. The faster the ball goes, the bigger the drag. The faster it goes, the harder it is to go fast.

Adding Turbulence

 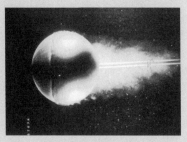

When air flows over a rough surface, the layers of air right next to the ball get turbulent—and that affects the ball's wake. The ball on the left is smooth; the ball on the right has a wire hoop around it. Like the stitches on a baseball or the dimples on a golf ball, the wire creates turbulence in the air. That turbulence helps the air stick by the ball's surface longer, making a smaller wake—which means the ball has less drag and can fly farther.

Stitches and Curves

The turbulence caused by stitches and dimples can also affect the direction of a ball's flight. A stitchless ball wouldn't curve in the same way familiar baseballs do.

To throw a curveball, a pitcher puts a spin on the ball as he releases it. The spin of the ball shifts the places on the ball's surface where the air becomes turbulent. That, in turn, causes the ball to engage in "preferential shedding." That sounds like the principle that white pets tend to nap on dark clothing, but in fact it refers to the way air shoots off the ball in one direction or another, thus propelling the ball in the opposite direction. Exploratorium physicists glibly refer to this as "the basic action-reaction thing," which is shorthand for Sir Isaac Newton's Third Law of Motion: "for every action there is an equal and opposite reaction." (See pages 84–85 for details.)

Without the stitches, a curveball might change direction a bit, but it would be hard to make it curve deeply and break sharply, which is what can make curveballs so devilishly hard to hit. (Sandy Koufax, who played for the Dodgers, was once said to throw a curveball that "collapsed at the plate like a folding chair.") And if the baseball had no stitches, it would be impossible to throw knuckleballs—those erratically fluttering pitches that have exasperated batters and catchers alike for decades. That means famous knuckleballers—like the Texas Rangers Charlie Hough, the New York Giants Hoyt Wilhelm, and the Cleveland Indians Satchel Paige—would have had to come up with an entirely different bag of tricks.

Lots of pitchers exaggerate the turbulence around a baseball by doctoring it, or enhancing roughness on one side of the ball or another. In the major leagues, doctoring balls has been illegal since 1920, but pitchers still do it. Joe Niekro of the Minnesota Twins created "sandpaper balls" with an emery board and sandpaper. St. Louis Cardinals pitcher Bruce Sutter created "shiners" by shining up one side of the ball against his uniform, making the rest of the ball comparatively rough. Rick Honeycutt, who started in the majors with the Seattle Mariners, once stuck a thumbtack through a Band-Aid wrapped around his finger and used the point to roughen the ball. All these players got caught.

Back in the late 19th century, golfers also discovered the advantages of roughening the surface of a ball when they realized their old, nicked gutta-percha balls (gutta-percha is a sap from a Malaysian tree) flew farther than their new, smooth ones. Before using a new ball, a golfer would hack away at it with a hammer to introduce a little surface roughness.

Dimples on a modern golf ball (or the scuffs and dents on an old gutta-percha ball) keep the ball in the air the same way that the stitches help a baseball fly: by creating turbulence, which reduces drag. Today's dimpled golf balls easily go 200 yards, where an undimpled one would only go about 50 yards.

The Physics of Knuckleballs

If you throw a baseball with little or no spin, the ball's stitches become particularly important. The air flowing past the ball can "hang onto" the ball's surface longer on the side with stitches than it does on the ball's smooth side. As a result, air leaves the ball headed in the direction away from the stitches. When the ball throws air toward the smooth side, the air pushes back on the ball in the direction of the stitched side and the pitch curves slightly toward the side with stitches.

Knuckleballs are thrown with little or no spin and they typically make only one-quarter to one full rotation during the entire trip from the mound to home plate (compared to an average curveball's 18 rotations). But because a knuckleball has some spin, the position of the stitches changes during the pitch, and so the direction in which the ball is pushed also changes. These constantly changing nudges make the knuckleball sink, skip, and swerve erratically on its way to home plate. It's hard to hit and equally hard to catch.

Why does spinning a ball make it curve?

The secret to understanding the curveball is the speed of the air moving past the ball's surface.

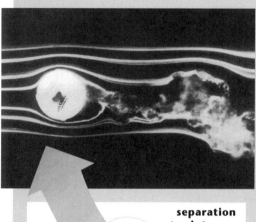

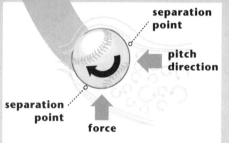

separation point

pitch direction

separation point

force

The ball in the photo is spinning clockwise, like a ball thrown with backspin. As the ball spins, its top surface is moving in the same direction in which the air is moving (from left to right in the picture). At the bottom of the ball, the ball's surface and the air are moving in opposite directions. So the velocity of the air relative to that of the ball's surface is larger on the bottom of the ball.

What difference does that make? Well, the higher velocity difference puts more stress on the air flowing around the bottom of the ball. That stress makes air flowing around the ball "break away" from the ball's surface sooner. Conversely, the air at the top of the spinning ball, subject to less stress due to the lower velocity difference, can "hang onto" the ball's surface longer before breaking away.

As a result, the air flowing over the top of the ball leaves it in a direction pointed a little bit downward rather than straight back. As Newton discovered almost three hundred years ago, for every action there is an equal and opposite reaction. So, as the spinning ball throws the air down, the air pushes the ball up in response. A ball thrown with backspin will therefore get a little bit of lift.

Now imagine that the photo was taken looking down from above on a ball spinning clockwise (rather than being viewed from the side). The ball would curve toward the right, toward third base, from the pitcher's point of view.

A major league curveball can veer as much as 17½ inches from a straight line by the time it crosses the plate. Over the course of a pitch, the deflection from a straight line increases with distance from the pitcher. So curveballs do most of their curving in the last quarter of their trip. Considering that it takes less time for the ball to travel those last 15 feet (about ⅙ of a second) than it takes for the batter to swing the bat (about ⅕ of a second), hitters must begin their swings before the ball has started to show much curve. No wonder curveballs are so hard to hit.

One important difference between a fastball, a curveball, a slider, and a screwball is the direction in which the ball spins. (Other important factors are the speed of the pitch and rate of spin.) Generally speaking, a ball thrown with a spin will curve in the same direction that the front of the ball (home plate side, when pitched) turns. If the ball is spinning from top to bottom (topspin), it will tend to nosedive into the dirt. If it's spinning from left to right, the pitch will break toward third base.

fastball   curveball   slider   screwball

The faster the rate of spin, the more the ball's path curves.

Baseball manufacturers can't mess with the number of stitches on a baseball—that number was established by the Major League Baseball Association. But golf ball manufacturers continue to experiment with dimple arrangements. "The ideal pattern, shape, and number of dimples is always a topic of hot research," says Bernard Soriano, assistant technical director at the United States Golf Association.

Putting a Spin on It

Spin also helps flying objects stay in the air longer. A good golf player's stroke with a seven-iron sends the ball away with a backspin of about 130 revolutions per second. This spin throws air downward, which pushes the ball up, keeping the ball in the air longer.

Learning how a ball behaves with spin is a crucial skill for athletes—and for spectators. The rule of thumb is that balls curve in the direction of the spin on their front face. Spin the face to the

Rates of Spin

Spin plays an important role in how balls and other flying objects move through the air. The following spin rates are in revolutions per minute:

Bullet	40,000
Golf ball	8000
Baseball hit by bat	2000
Curveball pitch	1800
Javelin	1440
Frisbee (thrown by pro)	960
Football (spiral pass)	600
Frisbee (thrown by amateur)	480
Discus	400
Knuckleball pitch	120

left, and that's where your ball goes—left. Whack a tennis with topspin, and it curves downward sharply. Give it some backspin and it lofts upwards.

Spin isn't always a good thing. "Hooks" and "slices" (in which a spinning ball careens to the left or to the right off the fairway) are the bane of golfers everywhere; they result from excessive sidespin. For a golf ball to fly straight and true, a golfer has to hit the ball with the face of the club, aiming in exactly the same direction that the club is being swung. If the club face is tilted to the left or the right, the ball gets a little sidespin, as well as the usual backspin. The two spins combine: the backspin helps lift the ball, but the sidespin pushes it off course in the direction of the sidespin.

In the mid-'70s, researchers in California's Silicon Valley invented a modified golf ball that had deep dimples only around the ball's equator and shallow dimples at the pole. This ball, which was called the Polara, and nicknamed the Happy Non-Hooker, was supposed to fly straight. The USGA ruled it illegal.

The Polara episode gets a lot of attention, primarily because the manufacturers sued the USGA for $1.5 million. (They lost.) Hundreds of other balls are tested and rejected at the USGA's headquarters in New Jersey every year. Some still go on the market. In fact, many golf balls on the market advertise non-slicing attributes, even though the best way to stop slicing is still to develop a good swing.

More Spin Doctoring

The wrong spin can make a golf ball curve, but the right spin can make a football fly straight. Technically, footballs aren't really balls at all, but are "prolate spheroids." This shape makes a football an interesting projectile: throw it so that it travels through the air sideways and the drag on it is enormous; throw it with the point forward and it cuts the air like a knife. To make a football fly high and straight, you want to keep the end pointed forward as it flies through the air.

That's where spin comes in. When a quarterback throws a football in a long pass, he starts it spinning at about 600 revolutions a minute. Because it's spinning, the football benefits from gyroscopic stability. That's the principle that a spinning object maintains its orientation unless acted on by a twisting force, like aerodynamic forces (lift and drag) or a combination of aerodynamic forces and gravity. In the case of the football, this means that the spinning football keeps its end pointed forward, rather than tumbling end over end.

Throwing a forward pass takes a special touch—spin the ball poorly and it will wobble and perhaps tumble from the sky. But even a well-thrown pass may have a bit of a wobble—in slow motion replays of long passes, you can sometimes see the end of the ball wobbling. At first glance, it may look like it's rolling around like a drunken sailor, but if you watch carefully, you'll see that the wobble is regular—the end of the ball is tracing circles as it flies through the air. The physicists call this *nutation,* and they say it's just one of those things that spinning things do.

Footballs haven't always been spun. Early balls were shorter, fatter, and heavier than today's balls, and football was more of a kicking and running game. But once the forward pass was put into play, manufacturers began creating lighter, slimmer balls that would fly better.

Gus Dorais, a Notre Dame quarterback, was one of the first to perfect the spiral pass. In a 1913 game against Army, he completed 14 of 17 passes for 243 yards, helping Notre Dame beat Army 35–13. (Knute Rockne, then a receiver for Notre Dame, caught one of Dorais's passes and claimed, "At the moment when I touched the ball, life for me was complete.") It was Army's only loss that season; the *New York Times* reported that Notre Dame had "flashed the most sensational football ever seen in the East."

You may have noticed that some perfect spirals are more perfect than others: the nose of the ball traces a perfect arc through the sky, rather than staying lifted up, or just horizontal, throughout the pass. Why some balls fly in that lovely arc and others don't is a sports and science mystery. Honestly, no one knows.

Spin also keeps Frisbees and discuses flying. The spin makes them gyroscopically stable; their tilt during flight creates areas of high and low pressure that keep the spinning disks aloft. The faster the air is moving over the surface of the Frisbee, the more lift is generated. That's why discus throwers prefer to throw into the wind. The speed of the oncoming wind adds to the speed of the air moving over the discus's surface, increasing the lift.

What Goes Up Must Come Down and Then Go Up Again

Balls don't just fly through the air. Lots of sports require them to bounce as well. Bouncing balls squash or deform when they hit a solid surface, and then spring back into their original shape. It's that springing back that pushes a ball up into the air.

When a ball deforms and returns to its original shape, it loses some of its energy to heat. That's why balls bounce a little lower each time they hit. A very bouncy ball deforms and returns to its original shape without losing very much energy to heat.

Rubber squashes and returns to its original shape without losing much energy because it's made of long, tangled molecules known as *polymers*. When a ball made of these tangled polymers squashes, the tangles straighten out temporarily. Then the molecules return to their tangled state—and the ball bounces back. Rubber balls that are filled with air also bounce easily and bounce high, because the compressed air acts as a spring, squashing and bouncing back to its original shape.

Frisbee Aerodynamics

As a Frisbee flies through the air, some air travels over the top of the disk and is thrown downward as it leaves the back end; the rest collides with the underside of the disk and is deflected down. In reaction to this combined downward shove, the air pushes the disk up, giving it lift. A Frisbee will generate lift even if it's flying upside down, as long as the front edge stays a little higher than the back. Angle the front of the disk downward when you throw it, and that is exactly where your Frisbee will go.

Spin gives the disk stability, and that allows it to maintain the angle that keeps it aloft. Wind tunnel tests and computer simulations show that the aerodynamics of Frisbees are actually quite complicated. Funny how such a simple-looking object can have such complex motion. And yet, even a dog can figure out where it will go.

The degree of bounce is called the *coefficient of restitution* (COR). The easiest way to get a feel for the coefficient of restitution is to drop a ball and compare the height of its first bounce to the height from which you dropped it. (To get the actual coefficient of restitution, you take the height of the bounce and divide it by the initial height, then take the square root of that number.)

If you drop a brand-new, modern-day tennis ball from a height of 6 feet onto a hardwood floor, it bounces back to a height of about 2.6 feet, a COR of about .66. Back in the 15th century, tennis balls were made of leather and stuffed with a variety of strange materials, including feathers, bran, and human hair. In an effort to compare a modern tennis ball to an old-fashioned bran-stuffed one, we took a plastic bag, stuffed it with bran, and dropped it on the floor. Plastic is different than leather and our measurements were inexact, but our bag, dropped from a height of 6 feet, bounced just a few inches. We'd estimate its COR at about .22.

For balls that are inflated, the air pressure inside the ball has a strong effect on how well the ball bounces. Next time you open a can of brand-new tennis balls, compare the bounciness of a new ball to one that you've been using for a while. Chances are, the new ball will bounce higher—as tennis balls age, the air pressure inside the ball drops, making it less bouncy. That's why tennis balls come in pressurized cans, to minimize the loss of air before the can is opened.

Ball manufacturers have experimented with changing the air pressure inside tennis balls in an effort to change the game. In 1995 and 1996, Dunlop provided slightly deflated tennis balls to the players at Wimbledon to slow their nearly 120-mile-per-hour serves and create more opportunities for volleys. It didn't slow things up much.

Putting a Spin on a Bouncing Ball

When a spinning ball bounces, it always bounces in the direction of its spin. If the top of the ball is spinning to the right, the ball bounces to the right.

Try spinning a ball when you drop it and watch how it bounces. The absolute best ball to use for this experiment is a Superball, but you can see the effect with a racquetball or any other bouncy ball.

The easiest way to drop a ball with a spin is to hold it between your palms, then move one hand up and one hand down until the ball drops. If you move the right hand up, the top of the ball will be spinning to the left and the ball will bounce to the left.

Spin also affects how a ball bounces. When a spinning ball bounces, it always bounces in the direction of its spin. Some basketball players have learned to use this principle to their advantage. When a ball with a backspin bounces off the backboard, it tends to bounce downward into the basket, rather than away from the backboard. The easiest way to put a backspin on the ball is to throw the ball underhand. In the early years of basketball, lots of players used this technique and free-throw averages were higher. In recent years, Rick Barry, who played with the Golden State Warriors and the Houston Rockets, was one of the few pro players to shoot this way; his free-throw percentage of .900 makes him one of the most successful free-throw shooters in the NBA.

The surface from which a ball bounces also affects its behavior. Fast surfaces, like grass, which is slippery, make tennis balls bounce fast, low, and a little erratically. Wimbledon is the most famous "fast" court; one reason volleys are so short-lived there is because the grass calls for power hitting. Slow surfaces, like clay, create more friction. When a spinning ball hits a rough surface, some of that spin can turn into speed. The ball spins a little less rapidly, but moves through the air a little faster. (A physicist would say that the rotational kinetic energy is transformed into linear kinetic energy.) Sometimes one court creates two different kinds of bounce. On older courts, you'll see that balls bounce lower if they land in the alley right near the net—that's because that area isn't as worn down and the surface is rougher.

Changing the Way the Ball Bounces

If you change the bounciness of a ball, you can dramatically change the very nature of the game that uses that ball. Consider baseballs. Before 1848, baseballs were actually quite bouncy, or "lively," as they had a rubber core and were only about three inches in diameter. Some teams racked up as many as 100 runs per game. Over the next 25 years, bigger and heavier balls were introduced. These were "dead balls," which couldn't go as far or

Experiments with Bouncing Balls

It's easy enough to measure the bounciness of a ball. Drop it from a height onto a hard surface and see how high it bounces. Comparing the height from which you dropped it to the height of the first bounce gives you a measure of the ball's bounciness, something that the engineers who design balls and the players who use them spend a lot of time worrying about.

You can also change a ball's bounciness by changing its temperature. Take two golf balls that bounce to about the same height. Put one in the freezer for an hour, then compare them again. If your golf balls are like ours, the cold ball will bounce about 70 percent as high as the one at room temperature. Cold balls don't bounce as well, which is why some golfers keep their spare balls in their pockets on cold days, hoping to gain an edge by gaining a bit of bounce.

Try the same experiment with two baseballs, and you'll discover that an hour in the freezer makes a baseball 10 percent less bouncy than a ball at room temperature. That's not as dramatic a shift as we found with the golf ball, but it's enough to make a difference between a pop fly and a home run—which is why teams have, over the years, frequently accused other teams of cooling the balls to deaden them.

In some games, the change in bounciness with temperature is taken for granted. In squash, for instance, players rely on the pre-game warm-up to warm up the ball along with the players.

as fast as lively balls. Lively balls were still in use, though, and choosing the correct ball became an important strategy for home teams. If you had good batters you chose a lively ball, which would go farther. If you had good fielders, you chose a dead ball and played in close.

In the 1870s, the ball became more uniform. But in 1910, Albert G. Spalding—who had been a leading pitcher in the National League and who founded one of the most famous sporting goods companies in the world—began making very lively balls with cork centers. Because these balls gave so much power to hitters, pitchers had to come up with new ways of fooling the batters. Spitballs, sinkers, and knuckleballs all came into fashion at this time—so did scuffing up balls with dirt or emery boards.

"The tradition of professional baseball has been agreeably free of charity. The rule is, 'Do anything you can get away with.'"

—Heywood Broun, sportswriter, 1923

There's some debate about what happened next. Some people say that in 1920, a year after the Black Sox scandal (in which Chicago White Sox players were accused of throwing the World Series to the Cincinnati Reds), the major leagues introduced a still-more lively ball, primarily to create a wave of home runs and lure disillusioned fans back to the ballparks again. Indeed, batters hit a slew of home runs, making the 1920s what one writer calls the "most glorious hitting circus in baseball history." In 1919, National League batters hit 139 home runs; in 1921, they hit 460. Babe Ruth himself, playing for the American League, hit 29 balls out of the park in 1919—then a major league record. The next year, he hit 54 out of the park.

Others say the ball never became livelier, that the real reason batting averages shot up was that baseball bigwigs outlawed any tampering with the ball that year, including scuffing it up, fraying the seams, or coating it with spit, tobacco juice, or slippery elm.

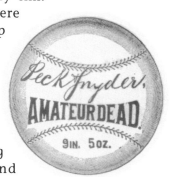

(Seventeen pitchers whose spitballs were their claim to fame were allowed to keep using the pitch; the last legal spitball was thrown by Burleigh "Ol' Stubblebeard" Grimes in 1934.) That gave the offense the advantage. Still another explanation is that batters were just learning to bat like Ty Cobb and Babe Ruth, that a relatively young game was just beginning to learn and practice skills.

Whatever the reason, the 1920s marked a new era in baseball. As pitchers gave up their spitballs, they carefully developed the curveball, which has befuddled batters and physicists for more than 70 years. Outfielders started playing farther back, and some of the more strategic offensive tricks of the deadball era, including stolen bases, hit-and-run plays, and bunts, faded away. Once the slugging began, those plays were no longer as vital for scoring.

Since then, there have been accusations that Spalding periodically introduces lively or "rabbity" balls by winding the yarn inside the baseball tighter. (Players have complained of balls being too dead only once, during World War II, when a rubber shortage forced Spalding to create a ball with a center core made of balata rubber, which wasn't as bouncy.) Spalding denied every charge. In 1925, *New York Daily News* columnist Paul Gallico suggested rabbity balls exist only in the eyes of the disgruntled beholder. He wrote that the "jackrabbit" ball is generally "a baseball that the other side is slugging something scandalous" and it's usually discovered by a team "that has been through a frightful shellacking." Experts have also posited other theories: that players are now using lighter bats, which allow for more swing and that players are getting more muscular.

What's inside a baseball?

Though baseballs are extremely hard and bouncy, they are made mostly of soft, pliable yarn. The balls used in the major leagues must meet precise specifications. If you wanted to make a ball suitable for the majors, here's how to do it.

First, surround a $^{13}/_{16}$th-inch cushion cork center with one layer of black rubber and one layer of red rubber. Wind this core with 121 yards of 4/11 blue-gray wool yarn. (The numbers specify the weight and number of strands in the yarn.) Wind about 45 yards of 3/11 white woolen yarn around that, wind about 53 yards of 3/11 blue-gray woolen yarn around that, and top that with 150 yards of 20/2 ply fine cotton yarn. Coat the ball with a special rubber cement. Make the cover of special alum leather and sew it on with 108 double stitches of 10/5 red cotton thread. The covers are hand-stitched, and it takes about 10 minutes for someone to sew the cover on the ball. When you're done, your baseball should be 9 to 9¼ inches in circumference and from 5 to 5¼ ounces in weight.

The strict specifications of materials is intended to ensure that all balls are created equal—no ball will be harder or softer or livelier or deader than any other. Today, balls are also tested to make sure they perform according to specified standards as well.

Physicist Party Trick

Here is one of Paul Doherty's favorite odd physics tricks. For this, you do need a Superball—accept no substitutes.

Throw the Superball under a table. If you get the angle just right, the ball will bounce off the bottom of the table, bounce off the floor, and bounce right back into your hand. You don't need to understand what's going on to give it a try, but if you want to know, here's Paul's explanation for the ball's strange behavior.

What's going on?

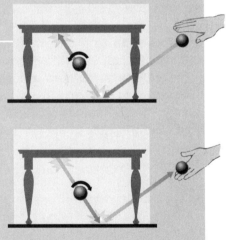

The ball leaves your hand with no spin to speak of. But when it hits the floor, it picks up a top spin.

When the ball hits the bottom of the table, that top spin causes it to bounce back in the direction that it came from. And that bounce off the table also causes the ball to reverse the direction of its spin.

That new spin means that when the ball hits the floor, it will bounce forward, right back into your hand.

The effects of spin and balance are exaggerated with a Superball because Superballs are a little sticky; there's a lot of friction between the ball and the floor.

Innovations Have Consequences

In a few sports, changes in materials have resulted in official calls for restrictions. Take, for example, javelin throwing. A modern javelin looks like a long stick with a pointy metal head and a funny corded grip, suitable for skewering saber-toothed tigers, but still kind of unwieldy. When thrown correctly, it flies high into the air, moving as fast as 75 miles per hour and as high as 65 feet.

In 1984, East German Uwe Hohn threw the javelin a record 343'10", considerably farther than a football field. That same year, a Norwegian thrower's javelin almost hit a group of judges watching a foot race on the other side of the field. Suddenly javelin throwing became a public safety concern.

Javelins were sailing farther than ever before because, over the previous 30 years, javelin designers had been designing aerodynamically optimal javelins, ones that had more surface area (and therefore could create more lift). Once the new styles were perfected, javelins regularly started going 35 feet farther than previous records.

In 1984, the International Amateur Athletic Federation dictated that the center of gravity for the men's javelin had to be moved forward on the pole and the tail had to be thickened. That reduced the javelin's lift, which meant it couldn't go as far. Distances immediately dropped by about 60 feet. Tom Petranoff, who had broken the javelin world record in 1983, told *Sports Illustrated* three years later, "It's like changing the height of the basket or the size of the baseball. It's really that fundamental."

But here's the rub: over the last ten years, throwers have learned to throw even these redesigned javelins considerable distances. In June of 1996, for instance, Jan Zelezny, of Czechoslovakia, threw a javelin 323 feet—a record for the new design.

"The new rules didn't quite work the way they planned," says Glenn McMicken, a spokesperson for the United States Association of Track and Field. McMicken was a track and field coach at Southwestern Texas State College in 1986. He says, "We were a little upset by the rule changes, but since then a new breed of athletes has figured out how to throw the new style. The officials are thinking right now. They're not sure what to do."

Golf ball changes have also provoked officials to cap innovations, partly to save the golf courses themselves. In 1898, Coburn Haskell, an employee of Goodrich Tyre and Rubber Company, introduced the rubber-core ball. These "Haskell balls," which consisted of a rubber core wound round with elastic threads and covered with gutta-percha, were so much bouncier, or livelier than earlier balls that golf courses had to be expanded to provide for the extended play—sometimes by as much as 100 yards per hole.

Throughout the next four decades, golf ball manufacturers kept winding the elastic thread tighter and tighter, until the USGA ruled in 1942 that the initial velocity of a golf ball could be no higher than 250 feet per second. In the late 1970s they passed another rule: that a ball hit by the Iron Byron (a club-swinging robot) at the USGA testing site could go no more than 286 feet. (Of course, under other conditions, with a tail wind and a hitter more powerful than Iron Byron, balls might fly farther.)

Today, there are all sorts of golf balls available, including balls with semi-liquid centers and solid-core centers, balls covered with "surlyn," and balls covered with balata rubber. CORs can reach an incredible .890. Experts continue to worry that many courses around the world are in danger of becoming obsolete, yet some ball companies continue to boast that their balls will fly farther—and eager golfers buy those balls. In truth, however, it's only the pros that can consistently hit balls far enough to make larger courses necessary. Most amateur players would be happy to drive the ball in the right direction.

5 The Search for the Perfect Whacker

BACK IN THE OLD days, sports—and sporting equipment—were simple. You took a ball-like object: a rock, a skull, or a pocket of leather stuffed with bran. You took a whacking object: your foot, a stick, or the left tibia of a woolly mammoth. And then you whacked the ball with the whacker. You might whack it up into the air, or you might whack it along the ground, but the whole idea was that whoever whacked it the farthest, the highest, or whacked it into yonder stand of trees won the game.

Sporting life proceeded in this way for hundreds of years. Sure, clever craftsmen created beautiful golf clubs of hickory. And someone, perhaps a cleric, figured out that a stringed tennis racket worked better than a solid tennis paddle. (Some of the earliest tennis pros were bishops who played to celebrate Easter and who, as early as 1287, reported that "their dignity would not suffer by a little volleying of a tennis ball" after Easter dinner.) But, in general, sports rewarded those with superior athletic skill, not those who had the nicest toys or the biggest corporate sponsorship.

How things have changed! During the last fifty years, scientists and sporting goods manufacturers have poured tens of millions of dollars into developing the perfect materials for the perfect shape and the perfect weight of the perfect whacker. A lot of design innovations came out of the aviation industry, which took off soon after World War II. But is it doing any good? It may not take a rocket scientist to see that skill may be more than equipment deep.

Anatomy of a Whacker

When you see a whacker hit a whackee, it all looks pretty simple. The tennis racket slams the fuzzy little tennis ball and it zooms off across the net; the kicker kicks the football and it sails up and (we hope) through the goal posts. The whole interaction between whacker and whackee takes only a fraction of a second and then all eyes focus on the ball.

In that brief moment of contact, a lot happens. First, both the whacker and the whackee deform. Take a close look at the ball in the photo on page 100, and you'll see what a ball looks like at the moment it is whacked. Depending on its material, the whacker is deformed too—the hardwood of a baseball bat develops a temporary crater; a tennis racket's strings arch backward and the frame bends. Then both the ball and the whacker pop back to their original shape, and the ball goes shooting off through the air.

Ball regulators, by the way, spend a lot of time analyzing that pop to make sure the ball returns to its round shape after being hit. The United States Tennis Association (USTA), for instance, regularly uses a manual vice-like contraption called the Stevens machine (invented by Percy Herbert Stevens) to squash balls until they're only one inch thick. After ten seconds, officials release the pressure and measure the ball to see if it's as round as it was before, give or take three-thousandths of an inch.

By hitting a ball, you can make it change direction. Most people think that the way to make a ball go farther in a given direction is to hit it harder. It's actually a little more complicated than that.

As physicists see it, there are six important factors that affect how far a ball (or any other projectile) flies when you smack it: the mass of the ball; the mass of the whacker; the speed of the whacker when it smacks the ball; the speed of the ball when it encounters the whacker; the angle at which the ball hits the whacker; and the coefficient of restitution (or bounciness) of the ball and whacker together (see page 110).

"I never blame myself when I'm not hitting. I just blame the bat and if it keeps up, I change bats. After all, if I know it isn't my fault that I'm not hitting, how can I get mad at myself?"

—Yogi Berra

All of these factors contribute to how far and fast the ball flies. When you're in the middle of a game, you can't do much to control the mass, the speed, or the bounciness of the oncoming ball. You can control the other factors though. Most importantly, you can control the speed of the whacker when it hits the ball. Changing the mass of the whacker makes a difference, but not as much of a difference as you might think.

Consider these calculations for golf. When a professional golfer hits a drive, the driver head is traveling at about 100 mph when it makes contact with the ball. The ball then flies merrily away at about 135 mph. Now suppose you doubled the weight of the head of the driver, from 7 ounces to 14 ounces. Swing the club at 100 mph again and the ball would fly away at 149 mph—a little faster, but not much. A ridiculously heavy 16-pound head traveling at 100 mph would only move the ball's speed up to 165 mph. Even a driver head weighing 10,000 pounds, traveling at 100 mph, would send the ball away at a measly 166 mph.

On the other hand, consider what would happen if you could swing that club a little faster. A driver head traveling at

100 mph sends the ball away at about 135 mph, but if you could double the speed of the club head and swing it at 200 mph, the ball would fly away at almost twice that speed—250 mph.

During a drive, the face of the golf club is in contact with the ball for only half a millisecond, just half a thousandth of a second.

Based on all this, you might figure that you should reduce the weight of the club head so that you can swing it faster. Unfortunately, reducing the weight of the head doesn't really add that much to the speed of the swing. Since you've got to swing the club shaft and your arms, and move other parts of your body along with the club head, cutting the club head's weight by 10 percent only adds about 2 percent to the speed of your swing. In the end, the folks at the Golf Society of Great Britain (after some thorough scientific studies) suggest that you choose the weight of your club head by feel and by trial and error.

In *Search for the Perfect Swing*, authors Alastair Cochran and John Stobbs sum up the Golf Society's conclusions when they write: "There is, in fact, a very wide range of club head weights which will give any player much the same length from the tee if he strikes the ball squarely. What weight of club head he should choose is thus much more a matter of what combination of weight and swinging speed suits his own individual characteristics and abilities in the practical matter of swinging consistently at the ball."

The same principles apply in other sports that

Physicist Party Trick

This trick from Exploratorium physicist Paul Doherty lets you add together the bounces of two balls and send one ball flying. When we tried this trick on the Exploratorium's exhibit floor, we gathered a crowd of visitors who wanted to know what we were doing. We explained that we were engaged in serious scientific experimentation related to energy transfer. Some of them may have believed us.

You need a basketball, a baseball, and a few other balls. We used a tennis ball, a softball, and a Superball. Drop a baseball on the floor and notice how high it bounces. It bounces a little, but not much. Now hold the baseball on top of the basketball.

Drop the two balls together and notice what happens. The baseball will bounce off the basketball and fly off over your head.

Try the same thing with the other balls you've gathered and see which one bounces best.

What's going on?

To get a feel for what's going on here, drop the basketball on its own and notice how high it bounces. Then drop the basketball and the baseball together and notice how high the basketball bounces. When you send the baseball flying, the basketball doesn't bounce as high.

How high the basketball bounces is an indication of how much energy (in this case, kinetic energy, the energy of motion) the basketball has. When the basketball sends the baseball flying, the basketball doesn't bounce as high because it has transferred some of its energy to the baseball. This may look like a party trick, but it's really an important demonstration of one of nature's fundamental laws: energy can't be created or destroyed. All you can do is move it around, change it from one form to another.

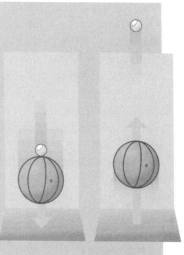

What does all this have to do with bats and rackets—or sports in general? When you bounce a baseball off a basketball, you are transferring energy from the deformation of the basketball to the baseball. When you bounce a tennis ball off a tennis racket, you are transferring energy from the stretching of the racket strings to the tennis ball.

Even though tennis balls and Superballs ordinarily bounce much better than baseballs, we found that the baseball actually bounced better off the basketball. How well a ball bounces off the basketball (or the strings of a tennis racket) has to do with timing. When the basketball hits the floor, it squashes a bit. When it springs back to its original shape, it pushes off the floor—it bounces. The baseball (or tennis ball or Superball) does the same. To get the maximum bounce when you're bouncing a ball off a basketball, you want the basketball to spring back to its original shape at just the right time to give the other ball a push as it springs back to its original shape. If the second ball squashes and springs back too fast, it'll already be gone by the time the basketball tries to give it a push.

involve whacking a ball. Terry Bahill and William J. Karnavas, engineers at the University of Arizona, did a detailed study of baseball players (ranging from Little Leaguers to professionals) and the speed with which they could swing bats of various weights. They found that the speed at which a professional player could swing a bat varied with the bat's weight—from about 50 mph to nearly 80 mph. They concluded that "the ideal bat weight varies from person to person," but generally they recommended lighter bats.

The angle at which the ball makes contact with the whacker affects the speed of the ball when it flies away—but it can have an even more important effect on the ball's spin. In the ruthless game of table tennis or Ping-Pong, spin caused by impact with the paddle plays a particularly important role. When a table tennis player drives the ball back at his opponent by swinging the paddle forward and upward, he gives the ball topspin. This topspin changes the way the ball bounces (see page 91)—the ball comes off the table faster than it hit the table and at a lower angle. That makes it tougher to return. Players may also bring the paddle downward and forward as they hit the ball, to put backspin on the ball, or they can put sidespin on the ball, making it bounce to one side or the other. Tennis players make use of the same principles to add spin to the ball and affect how it flies through the air and how it bounces.

So, whackers change a ball's direction, add spin and, if you hit the ball just right, make a great noise. These days, though, some wacky manufacturers are making whacker equipment that practically plays the game for you. In doing so, they've created a multimillion dollar industry and a heap of controversy.

What a Whacket

Until 1976, the USTA didn't really have any rules regarding tennis rackets. The association carefully regulated court size and ball behavior, but your racket could be "of any material, weight, size or shape." (One USTA official even said that players could use broomsticks with tomato cans on top.) Today, the length, width, and depth of rackets is restricted, as is the string pattern. But players still have a lot of room to experiment. You could play with a square racket with two strings, with a racket shaped like a donut, or even with a racket made out of doughnut dough, if you thought it would do the trick.

Of course, most tennis players want a tennis racket that actually makes it easier to hit the ball. For hundreds of years, since the 15th century in fact, tennis players had played with rackets that had wooden frames and strings made from the intestines of various barnyard animals. Then in the late 1960s, a funny thing happened: tennis got very, very popular. Tennis matches like Wimbledon and Forest Hills that had previously been only for amateurs became "open" to professionals: women stars like Billie Jean King and Chris Evert became symbols of the burgeoning feminist movement; networks discovered that tennis was a great sport to pipe into people's living rooms.

When a tennis pro smacks a tennis ball with a racket, the ball is in contact with the racket for four- to five-thousandths of a second. In that time, the racket imparts enough energy to the ball to send it flying away at something like 150 mph.

In response, thousands of people went out and bought nifty outfits, shiny new rackets, and cans of tennis balls. When they hit the courts though, many were disappointed. "Men who hadn't been out of long pants since they were six years old got out there in their white shorts and spent most of their time picking up balls at the back fence," says Brad Patterson, executive director of the Tennis Industry Association. "They looked like tennis pros, but they said, 'hey this is frustrating, I can't play this game.'"

Within five years, the tennis boom became a tennis bust. Then an engineer named Howard Head came on the scene. Head had already revolutionized skiing by making skis out of layers of aluminum and fiberglass, thus making them more durable and rigid. Soon after his 50th birthday, he decided to take up tennis. Lo and behold, like many other would-be tennis players, he had a tough time. So Head made a larger racket, one with a strung-surface area of 130 square inches, rather than the traditional 70 square inches. "People told him, 'you can't do that,'" Patterson says, "'It's against the rules.' But Head said, 'No, it isn't,' and he was right. Then people said, 'a racket like that will be too heavy,' and Head came up with an aluminum alloy design."

The glory of aluminum alloy is that it is both light and strong. Traditional wooden rackets had weighed about 12.5 ounces. Head's new racket, called the Prince, weighed only 10 ounces, so a player could swing faster and hit the ball faster, which makes the ball go faster. The strength made the frame stiffer, so less energy went to frame bending and more went to the ball. (See, the ball's only in contact with the racket for four or five milliseconds. If the frame takes 15 milliseconds to go back and forth, but the ball's only hitting the racket for four or five milliseconds, the frame can't impart its full motion to the ball. It's like trying to say good-bye to someone who's already hung up the phone.)

Head's racket design took off like a bat out of hell. Manufacturers began experimenting with large rackets made of all kinds of materials, including graphite and boron, both of which are several times lighter and stronger than wood. These new rackets had another thing going for them: a bigger sweet spot.

Most people know intuitively what the sweet spot is; it's that place on the racket that feels really solid when the ball hits it and makes a nice "whonk" sound. (In an informal survey, people also described the sweet spot sound as "thwonk," "whung," and "whop," while "thup," "pank," and "OW!" described the ball hitting someplace sour.)

That's the colloquial wisdom on the sweet spot. Physicists get a little more specific in describing it. In fact, they say, most whackers actually have three sweet spots.

First, there is the spot where the racket doesn't jump in your hand when you hit the ball. That means more energy goes into hitting the ball than making the handle scour out your palm. This is called the *center of percussion*. (See page 116.) Second, there's the spot on the racket that is the bounciest, or that sends your ball off with the most speed. (See page 110.) (One of the advantages of the Prince racket was that its coefficient of restitution, the number that measures bounciness, was .67, not the .57 of traditional rackets.) And third, there's the spot where your hand doesn't get a painful sting when you hit the ball. This is called the *node of the amplitude of the first harmonic*. It's the place where the sound waves created by the ball-racket collision cancel each other out. (See page 113.)

In an ideal world, all three sweet spots would be in the same place. Unfortunately, they're not.

In an ideal sports world, the three sweet spots would all be in the same place, located closed together near the center of the racket head, since that's where even beginners are most accurate at hitting the ball. Racket manufacturers have yet to design such an ideal racket, but sporting goods companies have made fortunes modifying tennis racket designs to bring the three sweet spots closer together or to increase the size of the sweet spot that provides the maximum rebound.

Changing the geometry and weight distribution affects the sweet spots. The head of an oversized racket, for example, has more string area closer to the handle than other rackets. This makes for a larger sweet spot of maximum rebound and a more popular racket for weekend hackers.

By developing lighter rackets, manufacturers moved about 60 percent of the racket's weight above

Maximizing Rebound

One of the three "sweet spots" applies primarily to tennis rackets. It's the place where the ball gets the maximum rebound power from the strings. It depends on how much the racket, the strings, and the ball deform as they collide. Since baseball bats and golf clubs don't deform much during impact with their balls, this sweet spot isn't important for them.

Sometimes called the power spot, this sweet spot is where the *coefficient of restitution* (COR) of the ball and racket combined is the largest. The coefficient of restitution can be defined as the ratio of the speed of the ball just after impact compared to what it was just before hitting the racket. The higher the COR, the faster the ball leaves the racket, and the more energy it gets in the collision. For the racket, the COR varies depending on where on the racket you hit the ball. It's lowest near the top rim (where the racket is most flexible), and highest near the handle (where the racket is stiffer). It also decreases as you move sideways out from the center line of the racket. That has to do with how much energy from the collision the racket absorbs and doesn't give back; the more flexible the racket, the more energy it keeps from being returned to the ball. Thus the third sweet spot tends to be centered in the lower part of the racket head, where the racket is stiffest.

To find the power spot on a tennis racket, lay it on a table with the racket face extending past the table's edge. Hold the handle down on the table and have a friend drop a tennis ball on the racket face from a height of about a foot or so, starting near the top rim and moving toward the handle. The COR sweet spot is where the ball bounces the highest.

Sweet Spots on a Tennis Racquet

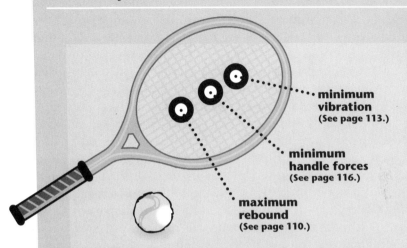

minimum
vibration
(See page 113.)

minimum
handle forces
(See page 116.)

maximum
rebound
(See page 110.)

How tightly should the strings on my racket be strung to be most effective?

Looser is better according to physicist and long-time tennis player, Howard Brody. Strings are designed to absorb (not lose) energy when they deform as the ball hits them. They give back almost 95 percent of the stored energy to the ball when they snap back into place. The more flexible the strings are, the more energy they can store. The ball, on the other hand, loses energy when it changes shape as it hits the strings. During the collision between racket and ball, loose strings squash the ball less, causing it to lose less energy. Thus they act as a better trampoline for the ball, sending it off with the most energy possible. One study found that the ideal string tension varies from 40 to 55 pounds. Professional tennis players often use higher tensions, but that's to increase their "control," not the speed of the ball as it leaves their rackets.

the center of the racket, which drags the sweet spot farther up. Such rackets are usually called "Super Light Head Heavy" rackets, which is the kind of name you probably shouldn't stare at too long. Patterson says the more appropriate name would be "Handle Light" rackets, since the racket is not really lighter, but the weight has been redistributed to put more in the hitting area.

By 1984, almost no professional tennis players were using wooden rackets anymore and the game had changed remarkably. A light racket in a strong server's hand can be a scary tool; the lightness and speed can make balls shoot at speeds of up to 150 miles per hour across the net; they're hard to see, never mind hit. One of the last pros to use a wooden racket was Bjorn Borg, who became the top player in the world in 1979 and 1980, using wood. In 1991, he tried to make a comeback at the Monte Carlo Open using his wooden racket. His opponent, Jordi Arrese, a 26-year-old Spaniard who was ranked only 52nd, used a graphite racket with a surface area that was 35 percent larger that Borg's racket. Arrese's balls went 30 percent faster than Borg's and he won 12 of 17 games. Bjorn Borg, as one of our physicists says, "got his clock cleaned."

Lightness, stiffness, and size seem straightforward. But in an attempt to make the perfect racket, people have come up with some really weird designs, including a racket with 100 little vials of metal powder embedded in its frame (to compensate for bad hits and reduce vibrations), a racket frame that was filled with liquid (to redistribute the weight as you needed it), a racket with lead shot in the handles (to absorb frame vibration), and even rackets with little beads and plastic worms on the strings (to dampen string vibration). All used physics as reasons for being. But if you imagine your opponent's reaction on the court ("My God, are those *maggots* on your strings?") you realize the edge may have been primarily psychological.

Today's standard racket is made of aluminum, graphite, or ceramic. It weighs about ten ounces and measures about 115 square inches. The frame is about 1.5 inches square. That means it's about 20 percent lighter, 64 percent bigger, and 116 percent thicker than rackets of twenty years ago. The new

Minimizing Vibration

When you hit a ball just right, you've hit it on one of the three "sweet spots" of the whacker. One of these sweet spots relates to vibration. Whenever an object is struck, it vibrates in response. These vibrations travel in waves up and down its length. At one point, called the node, the waves always cancel each other out. If you hit the ball on the whacker's node, the vibrations from the impact will cancel out, and you won't feel any stinging or shaking in your hand. Since little of the whacker's energy is lost to vibrations, more can go to the ball. The node sweet spot differs from the center of percussion sweet spot. (See page 116.) When a ball hits the node, you don't feel any vibration in your hand. When it hits the center of percussion, your hand doesn't feel any force pushing against it.

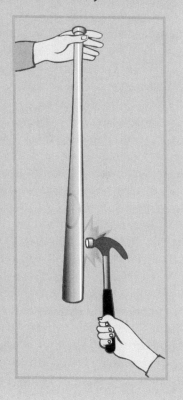

On most tennis rackets, the node is located about four or five inches above the center of percussion. To find the node on a baseball bat, hold the bat, hanging down, loosely between your thumb and index finger, just below the knob on the bat's handle. Have a friend tap the bat gently with a hammer, starting at the fat end and moving toward the handle. You should feel a vibration in your fingers whenever the bat is struck, except when the node is hit; then you'll feel nothing. You may also notice a slightly different sound when the node is struck.

rackets make it easier for amateurs to play the game. But some people are worried about how the new rackets have affected professional tennis; they feel that the game is getting so fast that it's no fun to watch anymore. The biggest point of contention is that serves, where the player can really send the ball flying, have become too dominant.

The International Tennis Federation has passed a few rules governing rackets. Those little beads are a no-no, for instance, because they put so much top spin on the ball that it's impossible to hit. The strings have to be flat and evenly spaced. And beginning in January 1997, the maximum racket length was reduced from 32 inches to 29 inches, in an attempt to slow the speed of serves.

Brad Patterson of the Tennis Industry Association says that there is disagreement within the sport about whether the game has become too fast. Even those who think the serve has become too dominant feel that this is a problem only in matches played by the male professional players on grass. "Only one tenth of one percent of all the tennis played is men's professional tennis on grass," Patterson says. "There are other ways to keep the serve from becoming too dominant. Instead of focusing simply on the racket, why not limit the players to one serve? Why not raise the net one inch?

"The perceived problem is only at the men's professional level. Almost everyone agrees that the women's game has been improved by the modern equipment. And certainly the recreational player has been helped greatly by the modern rackets."

Still, even some of the most famous pros wax nostalgic for the old days of varnished wood. In a *New York Times* interview in August 1996, John McEnroe said, "Why don't they go back to wood racquets? Then we would see the best tennis to be played. The most beautiful, consistent, best players in the world doing the best they possibly could. Instead of guys just going for broke on almost every shot."

Bats in the Belfry

Many people look to baseball as the model for how amateur and professional tennis players could divide their equipment. Although the traditional baseball bat is a pleasingly pure tool—a single piece of wood that's less than 42 inches long and 2¾ inches in diameter—today it's used only by the pros, while the amateurs get to play with the space-age equipment.

Batting, of course, is a tricky business. You have a slim, round piece of wood and a five-ounce ball hurtling at it at about 90 miles per hour. Generally, you have less than half a second to judge the speed and trajectory of the ball before you hit it. Misjudge the ball's speed, and you miss the ball entirely. Hit the ball even a few millimeters off the right spot on the bat and you hit a foul or a fly ball.

"Don't forget to swing hard, in case you hit the ball."
—Woody Held of the Cleveland Indians

The bat-ball collision is so ephemeral, in fact, that many players swear by ritualistic treatments of their tools. Some, like Eddie Collins and Cap Anson, left their bats outside to "season them." Ty Cobb oiled his with tobacco juice; others, like Honus Wagner, boiled them in creosote. To make his bat harder, Ted Kluszewski hammered nails into it. To make their bats bouncier, other hitters have hollowed them out and filled them with cork or Superballs. To add backspin, some players even carve little grooves into the bat.

Great stories, but according to the physicists, these methods probably don't work. Here's the problem. The wooden bat, while simple, is well designed for its job. As the batter swings the bat across his body, he pivots the bat, thereby making its tip go faster than the handle. That means the bat picks up a good bit of speed, as much as 70 or 80 miles per hour, in fact. When the bat hits the ball, which is coming at, say, 90 miles per hour, the ball deforms, staying in contact with the bat for about one millisecond before it pops back to its original shape and zooms off in another direction.

Minimizing Handle Forces

One of a whacker's three "sweet spots" corresponds to its *center of percussion* (COP). That's physicist talk for the point where the ball's impact causes the smallest shock to your hands. If you hit a baseball closer to the bat's handle than to the center of percussion, you'll feel a slight force pushing the handle back into the palm of your top hand. If you hit the ball farther out than the COP, you'll feel a slight push on your fingers in the opposite direction, trying to open up your grip. But if you hit the ball right on the COP, you won't feel any force on the handle.

A bat is essentially a long stick. When you hit a stick off center, two things happen—the entire stick wants to move straight backward, and it also wants to spin around its center. It's this tendency to spin that makes the bat's handle push back on or pull out of your hands.

When the ball hits the bat's COP, you don't feel a push or pull as the bat tries to spin. That's because when the bat spins, it pivots around one stationary point. When you hit a ball at the COP, the stationary point coincides with where your top hand is. So your hand feels no push one way or the other.

This is important if you want to hit the ball a long way. Every time you hit a ball at a point that's not the COP of your bat, some of the energy of your swing goes into moving the bat in your hands, not to pushing the ball so that it moves away from your farther and faster. If less of the bat's energy goes to your hands, more of it can be given to the ball.

When you hold a bat with your hands at the bottom of the handle (a normal grip), the COP is located about six to eight inches from the fat end of the bat. If you choke up on the bat, the COP moves closer to the fat end. That's because the location of your top hand is the place you want the bat to pivot. Changing your hand's position on the bat changes where that pivot point is, which therefore changes the position of the COP to one that corresponds to the new pivot point.

This doesn't just apply to baseball bats. All whackers have a COP. For a golf club, the COP is on the club face; a tennis racket's is generally close to the center of the racket head.

To find the COP of a bat or racket, hold the whacker parallel to the ground in your hand. Make sure you hold it at the same place you normally do when playing a game. It's easier to feel the push if you hold the whacker with only one hand; a two-handed grip helps to counteract the push in either direction. But be sure to hold it with the top hand in its "normal" position, no closer to the handle knob than you normally put your top hand. Close your eyes, so you can concentrate on the sensations you feel with your hand.

Have a friend throw a ball at the bat or racket from a few inches away, starting at the end farthest from your hand and moving down the whacker. The harder they can throw it, the better (as long as they're able to control where on the bat they're throwing the ball). Notice how the bat feels in your hand as the ball hits it. When we tried this at the Exploratorium, we could feel both a vibration and a force pushing on our hands. The amount of vibration and "push" varied depending on where on the bat the ball hit. Some of us found it a little hard to distinguish between the two feelings, but if you can, the COP is where you feel the smallest push on your hand.

minimum handle forces
(See page 116.)

minimum vibration
(See page 113.)

maximum rebound
(See page 110.)

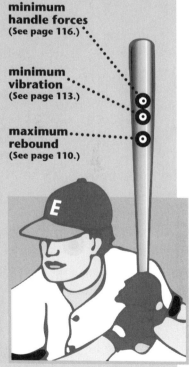

There's not a lot of room for improvement here. Adding nails to make the bat harder doesn't help because the bat is already so hard that the ball retains about 95 percent of its energy. In fact, more bat hardness would cause more ball deformation, which would make the ball lose kinetic energy. Carving grooves into the bat does nothing more than provide "occupational therapy," according to Robert Adair, author of the *Physics of Baseball*. (That's because the friction between bat and ball already adds backspin.)

Making the bat bouncy is equally futile; there's just not enough time for the cork to absorb the baseball's energy and then return it. Besides, once you open your bat to hollow it out, you automatically weaken it. Plenty of batters have had their bats crack open and spew either Superballs (Yankees Graig Nettles in 1974) or cork (Astros hitter Billy Hatcher in 1987, Cincinnati Reds Chris Sabo in 1996).

Still don't believe us? In an attempt to put an end to all this doctored bat business, Hillerich & Bradsby, who make the Louisville Sluggers, did a number of corking experiments, including filling bats with polyurethane foam. "We've found it doesn't affect hitting distance much at all," says George Manning, vice president of technical services. "There's a slight trampolining effect on the bat, but it's minimal, at best."

Foam, cork, and Superballs do add one important element: lightness. As with a tennis racket, lightness is critical for speed, which is critical for power. (In fact, some people say Hank Aaron hit so well because his small, quick wrists could snap the bat around.) Lightness also improves accuracy and timing.

Look Ma, No Hands

There is one problem with wood bats though. They break. A bat hitting a ball can generate as much as 8000 tons of force, which is a lot for a one-inch-diameter bat handle. Spraying cork on the catcher is embarrassing; flying bat fragments are downright dangerous.

In the late 1960s, several bat manufacturers started toying with non-breakable bat elements. The first to step up to the plate was Worth Incorporated, who introduced the first aluminum bat in 1969. These were light, they were strong, the sweet spot was bigger, and they didn't flex, which meant the balls went farther. By 1974, both Little League and NCAA baseball had adopted Worth aluminum bats. By 1979, Tennessee State Prison guards were armed with Worth's aluminum Tennessee Thumpers to bop prisoners who went bump in the night. Today, Easton, Incorporated, in California, is one of the leading manufacturers of aluminum bats in this country.

Easton also produces hockey sticks with aluminum and aluminum composite shafts and graphite or composite blades, again for the sake of lightness, stiffness, and durability. A number of top NHL players, including Wayne Gretzky, Paul Kariya, and Jeremy Roenick, use these newfangled sticks, but before they can get their mitts on them, they're tested by Easton's good buddy, "Robotski," a robot that hits high-speed shots while light sensors carefully measure the speed of puck and blade.

Aluminum is light and strong and it seems like the perfect material. But professional baseball players will probably never use aluminum bats. A professional baseball player wielding an aluminum bat could hit a ball so hard that it could kill a pitcher or a baseman. College students and minor league players get used to aluminum bats and often have a hard time making an adjustment to wooden bats once they hit the major leagues.

How important is my grip on the bat when I'm striking the ball?

You could let go of the bat when it strikes the ball and the ball would still go as far as it would if you kept the bat in a death grip. Of course, the infielders and fans might not like you very much, as they dive out of the way of your flying bat. But as far as the ball is concerned, you might as well let go.

That's because the time during which the bat and ball are actually in contact, and therefore, the time during which one can influence the other, is amazingly short—the entire collision is over in about 1.5 milliseconds (for comparison, the blink of an eye lasts 100 milliseconds). It takes at least 10 milliseconds for the information that you've hit the ball to travel the length of the bat to your hands and then be transmitted along your nerves to your brain. By the time you're aware the impact has occurred, the ball is already long gone. As a player, there's nothing you can do during the period of contact to affect the ball; it's physically impossible for you to react fast enough. All you can do is make sure your swing is the best it can be before you hit the ball. And don't let go before the bat comes into contact with the ball; then you'll lose energy, not to mention control.

How far the ball flies is determined by how fast the bat is moving when it hits. It doesn't matter how hard you grip the bat.

One solution to the problem of breaking bats could be a wood composite bat. These bats are covered with a layer of ash wood, but filled with foam and a reinforced fabric. They look like wood and hit like wood, but they don't break. In a Tufts University test, one such composite bat, called the "Baum" bat, showed no wear after 3000 hits, where a wooden bat usually breaks after 250 hits. And several companies have begun developing, and even marketing, bats made of such advanced materials as graphite composite, carbon cores, titanium, and ceramic.

Bat manufacturers have a whole host of fancy machines for testing their bats and batters. They have motion sensors, optical sensors, force sensors, strobe lights, and high-speed cameras. They have precision timers, mathematical models, and motion-analysis software. Louisville Slugger developers even go out to the desert periodically to shoot balls out of high-speed cannons and then take pictures of the ensuing collision of the ball with an aluminum bat. (The ball goes 160 miles per hour; the ball deformation, George Manning says, is "devastating.") But the information gathered by all this fancy equipment probably hasn't improved anyone's batting average.

Hitters like Ted Williams, Stan Musial, Roger Maris, and Hank Aaron had pretty darned good swings, and they didn't have the benefit of these fancy machines or fancy bats. In fact, it's been 55 years since any hitter had a .400 average (the last was Ted Williams in 1941). In the mid-1990s, there was a surge of home runs, which many blamed on excessively lively balls. But there may be a simpler reason: lighter bats.

According to bat manufacturers, bat weights have dropped from 40 ounces in the 1920s, to 33 ounces in the early 1990s, to about 30 ounces in 1997. This is partly because a whole new breed of players used aluminum bats on their way up and these players are used to lighter bats. And it's partly because some players are beginning to realize that a light bat confers power. Sure, some great batters used heavy bats: Babe Ruth swung a hefty 46-ouncer, as did Cincinnati Reds star Edd Roush. But Ted Williams, Stan Musial, Roger Maris, and Hank Aaron all used bats that were lighter than 32 ounces.

Today, some of the best hitters in the leagues, including San Diego Padres Tony Gwynn, Florida Marlins Gary Sheffield and Houston Astros Jeff Bagwell, are using lightweight bats. "No one uses a bat that approximates Ruth's weight anymore," Manning says. "It could be one reason for the home run surge." (Other possible reasons include batters who lift weights and outfield fences that are shorter.)

The Placebo Club

Golf, like baseball and tennis, has witnessed a veritable industrial revolution. For hundreds of years, golfers used wood for their clubs, including hickory, apple, pearwood, persimmon, and dogwood. In the 1920s, steel shafts became popular, which changed the game irrevocably. Steel is stronger than wood, so it didn't break as easily, and it didn't twist as much as wood either. With steel clubs, players could hit the balls farther. Steel clubs are also easier to mass produce than wooden clubs, which meant that for the first time in golf history, players could have matched sets of clubs.

Twenty years later, manufacturers started adding grooves to the clubs. This may sound like a small addition to non-golfers, but it was a big step for golfing kind. The grooves added more friction between the ball and the club head. This added more backspin, which made the ball go farther.

In the last thirty years, the major advances have had to do with materials and weighting. In the 1970s, Taylor Made introduced the first "metal" woods to be used by professional golfers. Since metal is harder than wood, the new club sent the ball careening off the club head faster. The metal woods distributed the weight differently too, so that it moved away from the center of the head and added a little more stability. That idea was expanded in the late 1960s, when mechanical engineer and golfer Karsten Solheim introduced first "toe-heel" and then "perimeter" weighting. Both of these changes basically enlarge the sweet spot so it takes up most of the club head. In fact, like tennis rackets, the entire club head has gotten bigger. Traditional clubs had a volume of about 150 cubic centimeters; today you can buy clubs with heads that range from 200 to 300 cubic centimeters.

Today, golf club designers incorporate all the lightweight materials that tennis racket makers do. Shafts are available in graphite, stainless steel, and boron for lightness and strength. Heads are available in plastic, wood, metal, nickel, and cobalt chromium. It is perhaps the makers of titanium club heads who have most shattered the illusion of golf as a simple pastoral game. Titanium was originally a military product, used to make B1 bombers and intercontinental missiles. Club manufacturers seem rather fond of these militaristic roots—advertisements for titanium clubs often claim that the clubs "kill balls on contact," "launch missiles off the club face" and serve as a "eulogy for stainless steel."

David Feherty, Irish golfer, after being paired with John Daly in the first round of the British Open: "He hits his divots farther than I hit my drives."

"We're in an era of designer materials," says Dick Rugge, Taylor Made's product development manager. "We're beating our swords into golf clubs now, not just ploughshares. And we're working our tails off to create golf clubs that people like. It's like the Manhattan Project down here." Some golf courses have even introduced hi-tech golf carts that make use of global positioning satellites to help golfers figure out how far the hole is. That's the same kind of technology that the Pentagon uses to aim their missiles.

A lot of professional players are less than thrilled with the new materials and head sizes, however. Some pros don't like the broader weighting, because they can't influence the spin of the ball as precisely. Many also miss being able to truly "feel" the sweet spot when they hit. "For amateurs, having a more forgiving club head is great because they get better results and better feeling from their less-than-perfect shots," Rugge says. "Hitting it smack in the middle is not a normal event for them. But pros who

Swings, Slices, and Hooks

The golf swing is a perfect example of how small actions can have large effects. A golfer swings the club's grip end through an arc of at most a few feet. Because of the club's length, the club's head moves along an arc of 12 feet or more in the same amount of time. This may not seem like anything to get excited about, but it makes a big difference in how fast the club head is moving by the time it hits the ball. Indeed, club heads accelerate about a hundred times faster than the fastest sports car. In as little as one-fifth of a second, the club head

goes from zero (at the top of the backswing) to 100 miles an hour (at impact with the ball)! That 100-mile-an-hour impact sends the ball hurtling away at about 135 miles an hour.

The club and ball are in contact for only about a half a thousandth of a second, or half a millisecond. That's not very long—it takes you 100 milliseconds to blink, 2000 times longer than the time the club and ball actually touch each other.

During the half a millisecond of contact, tiny differences in the direction the club face points can have an enormous impact on the ball's flight. At the moment of impact, suppose the club face is not exactly perpendicular to the direction in which the club head is moving. The resulting tilt will move the ball slightly across the club face during the collision, giving the ball sidespin and causing it to curve in flight. If, at the moment of impact, the club face points to the left of the direction the club head itself is moving, the ball will hook to the left. If the club face points to the right of the club head's direction of motion, the ball will slice right.

It doesn't take much tilt to have noticeable effects. A misalignment of just one degree is enough to cause the ball to curve about seven or eight yards from a straight line by the end of a 200-yard drive. A tilt in club face direction of a mere three degrees will send the ball careening off into the rough at the side of the fairway. No one ever said golf was easy.

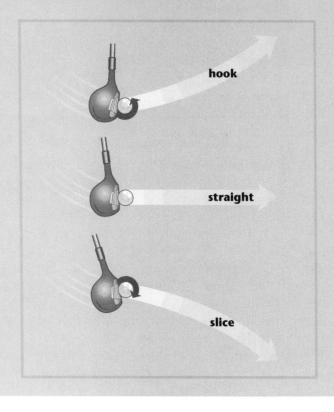

usually hit shots at the sweet spot want to know when they hit it off center. They need the feedback so they can quickly correct."

There have been innovations in club head shapes as well. There are clubs with holes in the head (to reduce drag); with mercury loaded in the head (to straighten the club face at impact); and clubs with laser beams coming out of the handles. There are clubs with "flow channels," "vertical stabilizing bars," "integrated quad systems," and "optimized cavity back designs." There are even clubs with a "short straight hollow hosel," which sounds like something those tennis-playing bishops might have uttered some years ago.

For all the aeronautic acrobatics, you'd think those little dimpled balls would be going to the moon. But they aren't. Over the last 25 years, neither professional nor amateur scores have improved much. Between 1968 and 1995, driving distances of pros only increased 12 yards, while the average winning score has fallen only one stroke per round per 21 years. Handicaps have fallen only one stroke in 25 years, and the professional record average of 69.23, set by Sam Snead in 1950, still stands.

"At the highest levels of play, like for the PGA tour, you don't see much change," Rugge says.

> "When it comes to sporting projectiles, golf is king. But what about baseballs? Basketballs? Footballs? Tennis balls? Forget about it. Nothing but concoctions of skin, bark, and hair. Where's the technology? In golf balls, that's where."
>
> —Steve Aoyama, Titleist Golf Company

"For the recreational player though, the benefits are clear. Playing golf is like playing a musical instrument. It takes a long time to get good enough to enjoy yourself. Missing the ball, or only hitting it ten feet is embarrassing. Better equipment helps lower the barriers to play."

Putters have gotten even weirder than other golf clubs. There are putters with mirrors (so you see the club and the hole), putters that stand up (so you can walk around and examine the ball's trajectory), a putter with a face that is angled down, to provide topspin, and a putter with a face that uses grooves to provide sidespin. For all those wacky designs, short games aren't improving either. According to a PGA study undertaken in 1990, even professionals have only a 50 percent chance of making putts from six feet, a 33 percent chance from 10 feet, and a 10 percent chance from 25 feet. Those statistics basically have remained unchanged since 1963.

"Talking to a golf ball won't do you any good. Unless you do it while your opponent is teeing off."

—Bruce Lansky

"It's really a difficult question," says Ron Sauerhaft, senior editor of equipment at *Golf Magazine*. "You also have to ask, 'are the courses getting harder? Are people practicing enough?' I think one reason that handicaps haven't fallen is because the courses really have gotten harder. If you play the courses of yesteryear with the equipment of today, you'd see handicaps fall a lot."

Perhaps the most important change is the level of hope. Dick Rugge, who himself uses titanium golf clubs, says, "There's nothing magical about a titanium head, but it's a better material for what I call the "Two *P*" reason. The first *P* is physics. The second *P* is psychology. It's comforting to have a bigger head. It makes you feel like you have a better chance of hitting the ball, which makes you relax, which makes you play better."

But no matter how fancy the equipment becomes, games, as philosopher Bernard Suit wrote in 1966, are "goal-directed activities in which inefficient means are intentionally chosen." That means we still have to hit the little ball with the little whacker.

6 Mind over Muscle

SPORTS OFTEN SEEM like a contest of physical skill—a test to see who is fastest or strongest, who has the steadiest eye or the most endurance, who can jump the highest or fling a projectile the farthest. But sports aren't just about muscles. They are also about the mind. Whether you're working towards running five miles or being an Olympic marathoner, staying on track requires self-discipline, concentration, 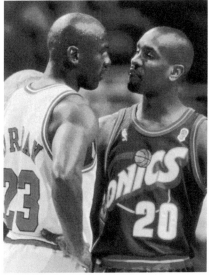 optimism, and some sense that your quest contributes to your individual pursuit of happiness. At the upper levels of competition, athletes' physical abilities may be very closely matched. It's the mental edge that makes the difference.

The Sports Shrinks

Athletes have known about the mental qualities needed to perform successfully for centuries. Those tennis-playing bishops in the 13th century probably knew intuitively that on days when the boss chewed them out, they probably didn't hit the ball too well. But it's only in the last 30 years that athletes and sports psychologists have really begun to break down what makes the athlete's mind tick.

Applied sports psychology first gained recognition in the United States in the late 1960s, when Bruce Ogilvie, then a psychology professor at San Jose State University, began working with professional football players in an effort to improve their performance. Today almost all pros, and many college-level athletes, use sports psychology. "If they aren't currently using it, it's almost guaranteed they've used it in the past, even if they are unaware that they have," says Dr. Diane Stevens, an assistant professor of sports psychology at the University of North Carolina, Chapel Hill.

Professional teams frequently have a sports psychologist on retainer. Sometimes the consultant works with the entire team, helping them to develop communication, team spirit, or clear roles for the team members. More often, they work with individual members to develop the psychological skills needed to give a really peak performance.

The issues that athletes face are pretty consistent, Stevens says. They need certain emotional coping skills, including motivation, an ability to set goals, relaxed responses to stress, and an ability to focus. Most athletes have some of these qualities; few have all. Many athletes, Stevens says, "are really good at beating themselves up. Athletes tend to be high achievers, so if they do something wrong, they tend to be very hard on themselves. They want to excel at everything."

One of the standard tools in sports psychology is visualization, or imaging, in which athletes mentally rehearse a certain movement (an effective forehand in tennis, for instance), a whole routine (whether it's a gymnastics performance or a football strategy), or having a relaxed response to a crisis (staying calm while your most dreaded opponent is beating the pants off you). No one's quite sure how the mental imaging actually affects the body—some think it stimulates certain neuromuscular links; others think it teaches the subconscious mind to take over during crucial moments. But many athletes use it now as a way to mentally rehearse their desired performance.

Visualization exercises aren't just idle daydreams about the perfect performance. They are usually carefully structured exercises that the athlete practices every day. (Most psychologists recommend a minimum of 20 minutes a day.)

If you'd like to try this at home, you can take a couple of different approaches. You can try conjuring up what you feel like when you're doing something really well: what the perfect forehand feels like or how you feel when you're running in a relaxed, rhythmic, and powerful way. Or you can visualize the moves of an athlete you particularly admire—how Janet Evans looks in the water, for instance—and then try imagining how those moves would feel if you were doing them yourself.

Sports psychologists suggest that you fill in the mental picture with as many sensory details as you can. Try to imagine the sounds that would be in your scene (the thunk of a ball on a racket, the cheers of fans, the splash of the water), the smells (hot dogs, a floor mat, a horse's sweat) and body sensations (the grip of the bat, the impact of your foot kicking a ball). "The more real the image, the more powerful its effect," Stevens says.

Such methods can be very helpful for either amateur or professional athletes. But elite athletes tend to focus more on "motivational" imaging than skills imaging. "Once you're an elite athlete," Stevens says, "you've got the skills down pretty well. So many of them image standing on the podium to receive their trophy, or hearing the crowd roar, or enjoying their medals. That can help keep their motivation and confidence up."

Just Relax

Learning to relax is crucial to sports performance because stress creates that "choked" feeling that can make athletes blank out, fumble, or simply give up. "Mental and physical focus is at the heart of competition," says Robert Mitchell, national rifle coach for the U.S. Olympic team. "In shooting, especially, being able to gain control of yourself while staying relaxed is key."

Some athletes, like speed skater Bonnie Blair, seem to thrive on high levels of stress. Others, like Dan Jansen, crumple. Reaction to stress is not just a mental thing. In one study, a Miami University researcher showed that the brain of someone trying to throw a ball while under stress sends conflicting signals to the muscles, which can throw off the person's performance. Other studies have shown that the hormonal havoc created by the body's natural response to stress can exhaust athletes at the very time they need the most energy.

"When we lose, I can't sleep. When we win, I can't sleep. But when you win, you wake up feeling better."

—Joe Torre, New York Yankees manager

Mental imaging can help athletes prepare for those high-stress moments when they think that they're losing or feel the fans are against them. "I tell people that their image will be like a guiding light for them in crisis situations," says Barbra Schulte, a personal performance coach who specializes in working with equestrians. "Let's say someone has an accident right before you go in the ring or you're very nervous about a certain competition. What you want to see in your mind's eye is your ideal performance. You want to be able to weed out the negative emotions."

Athletes use all sorts of other techniques to learn to relax, including "scanning" their bodies and progressively relaxing their muscles, meditating, or doing yoga. Some also learn to reduce the importance of an event, by realizing one loss won't ruin their career, cost them the support of fans, or otherwise destroy their lives. Others listen to music, control their breathing, or use positive affirmations to help focus on the task and not get distracted by rising anxiety.

In recent years, more and more sports psychologists have also begun using "talk therapy" to help their athletes. "We're realizing that giving them some visualization exercises, some stress management techniques, and some

Hot Hand and Hitting Streaks

Most basketball fans have watched players "catch fire," when it seems like every shot they take goes in the basket. Common wisdom has it that a player with "hot hands" is more likely to sink his next shot than would normally be the case. For some reason—more self-confidence, finding his rhythm, or some unexplainable influence—he can't miss. The problem is: common wisdom is wrong. There's no such thing as hot hands.

To understand this, we have to go back to the idea of random chance and the laws of probability. Think of a coin toss and the odds, or probability, that each successive toss will be heads or tails. You might think that if you haven't flipped tails for a few tosses, they're more likely to come up the next time you flip. But you'd be wrong. It doesn't matter what your previous toss was—heads or tails—or even what the last ten or twenty or a hundred tosses were. Your chance of flipping heads or tails is equal each and every time you toss the coin.

But what about flipping eight heads in a row? Surely that's something special. Actually, no. Runs—be they tossing heads one after another or making a string of successful basketball shots—are much more common than people realize. Try flipping a coin a hundred times and writing down whether it's heads or tails. You'll no doubt find a few seemingly amazing runs of all heads or all tails within the hundred tosses. But there's nothing unusual going on; such runs are predicted by the laws of probability.

The chances of flipping eight heads in a row (out of 100 tosses) is much higher than you'd expect—about 30 percent! It's almost a sure bet you'll get at least one string of six in a row. It has nothing to do with being in a zone or finding the right flipping rhythm. It's just what you'd expect from random chance and the laws of probability.

Stanford psychologist Amos Tversky analyzed every basket

made by the Philadelphia 76ers for more than a year. He found that the odds of a player making a second basket after a successful shot were no higher than predicted by random chance. In addition, the number of successful baskets in a row (a hot streak) were completely within the range expected by the laws of probability.

It's very human to look for patterns everywhere. We assign meaning to the patterns we find, even when there's no real pattern there. We see a player sink a few shots in a row and assume it's something unusual. But it's not.

Of all the streaks in sports, only one is extraordinary: Joe DiMaggio's 1941 hitting streak, during which he got at least one hit in each of 56 consecutive games. Ed Purcell, a Nobel laureate in physics and a baseball fan, analyzed all the streaks in baseball and figured out there's no way DiMaggio's string of hits could have occurred simply by chance. All of which makes DiMaggio's record an even more impressive accomplishment, perhaps even the single most amazing feat in American sports history.

motivational exercises may not be enough," Stevens says. "So many of us try to talk to every member on the team to find out what's going on in the rest of his life. We need to get to know the athletes' particular needs."

Strange Perceptions

Once athletes get mind and body working together, some claim that strange, almost superhuman things start to happen. Some runners claim they can see their own cells and organs. Sailors report being able to see the color of air currents, and golfers report seeing holes the size of washtubs. Some players, like Joe Namath, Bobby Orr, and soccer's Pele, seem to be able to see what is happening on the entire field at once. Others claim to be able to predict plays or moves ahead of time.

Stan Musial went so far as to say he could calculate the speed of a pitched ball when he was at bat. "Every pitcher has a set of speeds. I mean, the curve goes one speed and the slider goes at something else. Well...if I concentrate real good, I can pick up the speed of the ball about the first 30 feet it travels. I know the pitcher and I know his speeds."

Is that physically possible? Just barely. A ball takes about a half-second to go from the pitcher's mound to the batter. The batter has to start swinging right about the time the ball crosses the halfway line, which means that in the first quarter second of the pitch he has to judge the ball's speed and trajectory and decide how to swing at it.

Some athletes do have extraordinary powers of perception. (Ted Williams, for instance, had 20/10 vision; John McEnroe has 20/15.) But extraordinary skills can be better explained by experience than by heightened perception. "Batters learn to pick up pitches as they're being thrown," says Dave Barker, the Exploratorium's resident baseball aficionado. "To throw a curve, the pitcher has to spin the ball really fast. The curve ball rotates so fast that the red seams create a dark red spot in the middle of the ball. It takes practice to see this, but it's a really good clue." Outfielders also learn to field balls by analyzing the angle of their trajectory off the bat or by listening to the sound of the bat hitting the ball.

Other athletes learn similar skills. Riders learn to anticipate when a horse is about to buck or bolt by the animal's subtle ear and head positions, the rhythm of the horse's stride, the sound of his breathing, and the muscle tension in his back. Boxers and karate students learn that certain foot, shoulder, and eye movements presage a hit or kick; badminton and tennis players sometimes perceive a subtle movement in the opponent's chest. Athletes may not always know exactly what tells them to expect a certain move or play or pitch, because they learned to pick up subtle cues at an unconscious level.

But sometimes what the players are seeing, and learning to respond to, isn't even what's happening. Consider the rising fastball. From the batter's perspective, this pitch rockets toward

How does Michael Jordan manage to hang in the air for so long when he goes up for a slam dunk?

Actually, he doesn't hang in the air any longer than any other basketball player. It just looks that way. Once he leaves the ground, Jordan is governed by the same laws of physics as the rest of us. How high he jumps depends entirely on how much force he generates with his legs as he leaves the ground. And how long he stays aloft is directly related to the height of the jump: the higher the jump, the longer he stays in the air.

A vertical jump of four feet leads to a hang time of one second. That's an unusually high jump and, it turns out, most basketball players, including Michael Jordan, don't jump that high. A three-foot-high jump has a hang time of 0.87 seconds. All the artistry of a slam dunk takes place in just eight- or nine-tenths of a second!

Jordan makes it seem longer because he holds onto the ball longer than other players before shooting or dunking, waiting until he's on the way down to let go of the ball. His tendency to pull his legs up as the jump progresses also makes it seem like he's staying higher than he really is.

Next time you watch the Bulls play, try to time how long Jordan stays aloft and compare it to other players' hang times. You'll see there's not much difference.

the batter, and then, right at home plate, jumps upward as if to skip happily over the swinging bat. According to physicists, a ball can't actually perform that gravity-defying maneuver. What the batter is really seeing is an optical illusion generated by a combination of visual clues and mental miscalculation.

Here's how it works. Scientists studying the eye movements of batters found out that often a batter tracks a pitch as it comes toward him—then his eyes jump to where he thinks the ball will cross home plate. His guess as to where the ball will be is based on how far the ball is from him, how fast it's traveling, and how much it will drop before it reaches him. He puts all that together and estimates where the ball will be, then swings his bat to connect.

Sounds logical, right? Sure, but that's a lot of calculation and that may be where the illusion comes in. Suppose the batter underestimates the ball's speed—maybe because the pitcher threw a couple of 80-mph balls before sending a sizzling 95-mph ball his way. Because the batter thinks the ball is traveling slower than it is, he also thinks it's farther away than it is—and therefore that it's going to have more time to drop before it reaches him. Then his eyes jump to where he thinks the ball will be, but the ball is closer than he thought, so it hasn't had time to drop and so it's higher than he expected. Or suppose the ball is spinning fast enough to gain a little more lift than the batter expected. Again, the ball will be higher than he thought it would be. Rather than realizing that his estimates were off, the batter puts these bits of visual information together and sees the ball jump upward.

Doesn't the batter ever learn what's really happening? Probably not. The brain and the eyes put things together on an unconscious level, so you can't talk yourself out of an optical illusion. Next time you see a mirage on the horizon, for instance, try to make it go away by reasoning with your vision. You could stand there for hours and it won't go away until the sun moves. It's even harder when the optical illusion is moving at you quickly; there just isn't time for a philosophical or physiological debate.

In the Zone

Often, the heightened perceptions associated with sports occur when the athlete is in a frame of mind where the body is working beautifully and the mind is peaceful, yet alert. Runners will report feeling weightless and inexhaustible. Riders report feeling at one with their horse. Rowers claim the boat and the crew functioned as a single unit, and tennis players report being aware of nothing except the ball and the racket face. Sports psychologists call this being "in the zone."

Some athletes report feelings of well-being so deep they border on religious feelings. *In the Zone: Transcendent Experience in Sports*, by Michael Murphy and Rhea A. White, quotes a number of players who claim to have had such feelings while playing. When Steve McKinney broke the world downhill ski record, for instance, he claimed, "I discovered the middle path of stillness within speed, calmness within fear, and I held it longer and quieter than ever before." Other athletes report feeling that some "higher power" helped them hit the ball, make baskets, or receive passes.

Sports psychologists have varying explanations for the feelings that come when an athlete is "in the zone." That feeling of flow, or transcendence, may be in part due to very high levels of concentration (this may be similar to a state of deep concentration that the Buddhists call *samadhi*). It could also be due to the rush of adrenaline and sugar that hits the body when it responds positively to a challenge. Or it may be due to a very fortuitous combination of emotional qualities, including "calm, control, focus, energy, and enjoying yourself," says equestrian consultant Barbra Schulte. "When it all comes together, everything feels like it's working together in harmony." While most of us probably go out for a game or for exercise with the vague hope that such a feeling will come upon us, Schulte says, "an athlete can be trained to bring those feelings up at will. In fact, sometimes just acting the part—by arranging our body to look the way it does when we're in the zone—can help bring it on."

Adrenaline Rush

Some sports activities—hang gliding, skydiving, rock climbing, scuba diving, marathon running, boxing, springboard diving, and daredevil skiing—routinely take their participants into exhausting, potentially injurious, and stressful situations. This elicits immediate and powerful physiological and psychological changes, usually called the "fight or flight response." Your body doesn't know if you're trying to reach a mountain summit, or if you're about to be eaten by a tiger. It just knows you're feeling stressed. So it makes sure you're ready to fight or run away, to face whatever might happen next.

As you rush toward the edge of a cliff with your hang glider, your brain signals your adrenal glands to produce *epinephrine*, commonly called adrenaline. You feel its effects almost immediately, the so-called adrenaline rush. Epinephrine increases the skeletal muscles' ability to respond quickly. It speeds up the breakdown of body fats into sugars, which the muscles need for energy, increases respiration to burn those sugars, and increases blood circulation to get the energy where it's needed most. It also relaxes some of the muscles of your internal organs and contracts others—which is why you feel "butterflies" in your stomach. This initial energy boost is rather short-lived, however, since epinephrine is burned up quickly in your system.

The adrenal glands also produce *cortisol,* a steroid hormone that continues the increased production of energy-full sugars after the epinephrine has been used up. It increases the rate of absorption of the sugar glucose from the blood by the brain and skeletal muscles, and decreases its absorption by other organ systems. In effect, you temporarily feed your brain and muscles and starve your other organs. This allows you to function on very limited energy reserves, with most of the energy directed where it's most needed. But your body pays for this borrowed energy later.

Cortisol also suppresses inflammation and swelling in response to tissue damage, so you aren't impaired by pain or immobility. This may be why some athletes can continue to play even after rather serious sprains; the cortisol temporarily masks the symptoms. Heightened cortisol levels can continue in your body long after a crisis has passed, and are part of the reason you feel exhausted when it's all over. Ultimately, cortisol helps shut down the stress-activated systems, bringing you down off the hormonal high your body thought it needed to survive.

If you engage in stressful activity on a regular basis, however, your body adapts over time. The more you engage in a risk-taking, stress-inducing sport, the less will be the overall hormonal high. You need to do something just a little riskier each time to get the same experience. So athletes and risk-taking sports participants constantly push themselves toward new challenges and records, in part, to maintain that same adrenaline rush.

The Great Psych-Out

Of course, no one wants the other guy to even get one little toe in the zone. Athletes use all sorts of tools to break the concentration, focus, and confidence of their opponents. In some cases it may be appearances; Ken Caminiti, for instance, a third baseman for the San Diego Padres, is nicknamed Scary Man, because of the fierce game face he puts on before stepping up to bat. Hockey players paint their helmets with animals and elaborate designs to ward off the puck and scare the other players. Ty Cobb used to glare at pitchers to throw them off. And Green Bay Packer Tony Mandarich has a tattoo that says "appetite for destruction."

Athletes also use language to throw their opponents off. For years, professional basketball players have been using "trash talk"—a kind of drive-by verbal provocation. The goal is to distract or infuriate the other guy enough so that he loses his concentration or physically attacks you, which gets him ejected from the game. Insults range from taunts about other players' skills (Sam Jones, for instance, used to murmur "too late baby," as he shot the ball over Wilt Chamberlain's

outstretched fingers) to ethnic slurs (Yugoslavian Drazen Petrovic was once accused of partaking in the World Trade Center bombing). One of the earliest practitioners, and a true grand master of trash talk, was Boston Celtics Larry Bird. He once taunted Julius Erving by murmuring the two men's respective shooting totals, "36-5, Doc, 36-5," until Erving finally lost his cool and jumped Bird.

Knock Wood and Never Wash Your Socks

Some superstitious athletes try to affect the game in a different way: through ritual behavior. Yankees third baseman Wade Boggs eats chicken, and then goes through a carefully choreographed four-hour routine on the field before each home game. Ed Eyestone, a two-time Olympic marathoner, refuses to let his wife wear aqua on the day he races, because he performed poorly the three times she has worn that color. Art Larsen, the U.S. Open tennis champion in 1950, was nicknamed "Tappy" because he believed that tapping on objects with his racket—including the baseline, the net, and the umpire's stomach—would give him good luck.

Sometimes the entire team participates in a particular effort. Teams that are winning often agree not to wash uniforms—the Salt Lake Trappers of the Class A Pioneer League refused to wash their socks during a 29-game winning streak in 1987. When the San Francisco Giants went through a 10-game losing streak in the summer of 1996, the players started hiking up their pant legs. (The day they won, manager Dusty Baker had sprinkled good luck rice on the pitcher's mound.) The San Francisco 49ers began winning games in 1995 when they wore old-fashioned uniforms. They asked—and received—special dispensation from the NFL to keep wearing the uniforms. And former Oakland Raiders coach John Madden used to keep his players in the locker room until running back Mark van Eeghen had burped.

There are some sport-wide superstitions too. Many hockey players feel they have to tap the shins of their goalie with their sticks before starting a game. Most baseball players take pains to step over (and not on) chalk lines on the field. And there's an unspoken agreement that no one in the dugout will mention a no-hitter in progress.

Where do they get this stuff? Some superstitions are derived from ancient beliefs—avoiding chalk lines probably comes from the childhood rhyme: "Step on a crack and you'll break your mother's back." Not washing uniforms derives from an ancient superstition that bathing washes away good luck. Other superstitions are passed down from one generation of players to the next. But generally, people grab onto superstitions in the hope that their puny actions can garner them some control over what seem like the random events of life or to give them some edge over what seem impossible odds on the field.

But couldn't there be some cosmic link between our little rituals and the machinations of the Great Umpire in the Sky? Probably not. (Show us an athlete who has never, ever lost or fumbled while doing "the right thing" and we'll consider a different position.) More likely what happens is what psychologists call a "coincidental reward." That is, we do something, like wear a certain shirt, and that day we perform well. The next week, we wear the same shirt and we do well again. The week after that, we wear a different shirt and we fall on our faces. Voila! A superstition is born. From that day forward, most of us would wear that same shirt, even if we lost sometimes while wearing it.

What can make rituals even more powerful is the fact that once we believe them, we feel funny if we don't complete them, and that funny feeling can throw off our performance. Let's say, for instance, that you always wear the same pair of Calvin Klein underpants when you play volleyball. Suppose that one day you decide to live dangerously and wear a different pair of underpants. You may start to worry about what you've done once you get out on the court. Maybe the new underpants don't feel right, or you start second-guessing your decision. If that happens, then your mind isn't focused on the game and you're not feeling particularly relaxed or confident. In fact, you're a bit preoccupied. That may very well affect your performance.

> "I have only one superstition. I make sure to touch all the bases when I hit a home run."
> —Babe Ruth

Moral of the story? Wear your lucky clothing or complete your lucky ritual before you play. It may give you a psychological edge by helping you relax.

Psychology of Fans

Of course, sports aren't just for athletes; they're also for the fans. And fans are notorious for getting deeply, heavily, and sometimes irrevocably involved in their favorite team's performance. They shout with jubilation when their team scores; they swear when a particular team member makes a mistake; they weep when the team loses a playoff. Armchair shrinks might quip that it's merely athlete wanna-bes trying to live out their dreams. Sports psychologists say it may be something more: it's a way of feeling part of a larger community.

Feeling like part of a group has proven benefits: it helps reduce stress and boost confidence, for instance. That's one reason fans love sports jargon, stats, and biographies. Feeling deeply connected to the team is also a way of feeling deeply connected to the broader universe. That's also why so many fans indulge in their own rituals—wearing a certain shirt for the playoffs, for instance, sitting only in certain seats, changing seats to change the team's luck, or always eating the same food. Fans at home also have rituals to make them feel a part of things—refusing to leave the room except during commercials, yelling "no" when an opposing team tries to score, or scrupulously refusing to read or channel surf during important games.

Does any of this have an effect on a team's performance? Even scientists ponder these mysteries. In *Boojums All the Way Through,* for instance, physicist N. David Mermin wrote, "I'm a New York Mets fan, and when they play a crucial game I feel I should watch on television. Why? Not just to find out what's going on. Somewhere deep inside me, I feel that my watching the game makes a difference—that the Mets are more likely to win if I'm following things than if I'm not. How can I say such a thing? Do I think, for example, that by offering up little prayers at crucial moments I can induce a very gentle divine intervention that will produce the minute change in trajectory of bat or ball that makes the difference between a hit or an out? Of course not! My feeling is completely irrational."

To really look into whether Mermin was being irrational or not, we'd have to have a pretty heated and heavy conversation about quantum mechanics, probability theory, observer-induced realities, and metaphysics. We're not going to do that. Suffice it to say that right now there is no scientific evidence that you can instantaneously affect a team's score, a player's performance, a whacker's force, or a projectile's trajectory by saying a little prayer, sitting in certain seats, shouting at the television screen, or reading the newspaper during a game. (Even crossing your fingers won't help.)

You should still do that stuff if it makes you feel good, though. As Exploratorium physicist Thomas Humphrey says, "Even though I know my actions don't affect the game, I too can vocalize my support for a team very enthusiastically when it is doing something good. The human instinct to do such things is clearly very strong, even when we know better. In fact, one reason we shout at the television may be because evolutionarily we still can't tell the difference between the TV monitor and real life. We just can't restrain ourselves."

Of course, sometimes feeling part of the larger whole just makes the fans feel worse. If you're heavily identified with the team, for instance, their winning or losing can have a pretty drastic effect on your mood. Different fans identify with different teams to different degrees—that depends on the fan's personal history, his or her genetic makeup, and, sometimes, who's playing on the team. (If all your favorite players go to new teams, for instance, you may just lose interest in the original team altogether.) People who aren't highly identified with a team can watch and root, but not be devastated if the team doesn't win. People who come to see the team as an extension of their own egos, however, will see the team's performance as a reflection on themselves.

This may be one reason why fans sometimes get violent at competitions. The noise, crowds, heat, and competition arouse aggression in humans, especially if they already have a predisposition to hostility. According to researchers at the University of Kansas, when a deeply identified fan's team loses, the fan will experience a certain loss of self esteem. And aggression, it turns out, is an excellent balm for low self-esteem. But aggression also tends to dampen our cognitive abilities. So just as the hostile fan is feeling his worst, he's also making bad decisions: like deciding to call a fan of the winning team an idiot. Since team fans tend to identify with each other, once the brawl starts, most everyone will jump in.

Reactions may be partly hormonal too. Several studies have shown that testosterone levels tend to spike in athletes who win a game, whether it's football or chess. And testosterone has long been linked to aggression in men. But now researchers have found that watching a game—even on television—can make testosterone surge. In a study of soccer fans at the 1994 World Cup, Georgia State University researchers found that the testosterone levels of supporters of the Brazilian team, which won, went up 28 percent over pre-game levels. Testosterone levels of fans of the Italian team, which lost, dropped about 25 percent. Such testosterone surges may be linked to rioting at games and even the increase in domestic violence following especially emotionally wrought football games, like the Super Bowl.

"The lethargy and dull despair that accompany a losing streak can't be dismissed completely except by winning."

—Heywood Broun, sportswriter

Perhaps the armchair psychologists have a point though. Perhaps the greatest thrill of being a fan truly is that sense of living out our own dreams by watching others. Athletic competitions showcase beauty, grace, power, determination, and speed. That's obvious in figure skating or gymnastics, thoroughbred racing or the javelin throw. But even the most "violent" sports, like football, boxing, and hockey, begin to look beautiful as we learn to watch the individual players, the team's strategies, or the dance between opponents. Those are the experiences that engender joy, even exhilaration, for athletes and spectators alike. And those are the experiences that bring us back to the sports arena over and over again.

Sources

Adair, Robert K., *The Physics of Baseball.* New York: Harper and Row, 1990.

Armenti, Angelo Jr., ed., *The Physics of Sports.* Woodbury, NY: American Institute of Physics, 1992.

Baker, William J., *Sports in the Western World.* Lanham, MD: Rowman and Littlefield, 1982.

Blanding, Sharon L. and John J. Monteleone, *What Makes a Boomerang Come Back: How Things in Sports Work.* Stamford, CT: Longmeadow Press, 1992.

Brancazio, Peter J., *Sport Science.* New York: Simon & Schuster, 1983.

Brody, Howard, *Tennis Science for Tennis Players.* Philadelphia: University of Pennsylvania Press, 1987.

Cochran, Alastair and John Stobbs, *Search for the Perfect Swing.* Chicago: Triumph Books, 1986.

Colwin, Cecil M., *Swimming into the 21st Century.* Champaign, IL: Human Kinetics Publishing, 1993.

Easterling, K. E., *Advanced Materials for Sports Equipment.* New York: Chapman and Hall, 1993.

Ecker, Tom, *Track and Field Dynamics.* Los Altos, CA: Tafnews Press, 1974.

Flatow, Ira, *Rainbows, Curveballs, and Other Wonders of the Natural World Explained.* New York: Harper and Row, 1989.

Henderson, Robert W., *Ball, Bat and Bishop: The Origin of Ball Games.* New York: Rockport Press, 1947.

Jorgensen, Theodore P., *The Physics of Golf.* Woodbury, NY: American Institute of Physics, 1994.

Martin, John Stuart, *The Curious History of the Golf Ball, Mankind's Most Fascinating Sphere.* New York: Horizon Press, 1968.

Ryan, Joan, *Little Girls in Pretty Boxes: The Making and Breaking of Elite Gymnasts and Figure Skaters.* New York: Warner Books, 1995.

Schlossberg, Dan, *The Baseball Catalog.* New York: Jonathan David Publishers, 1989.

Schrier, Eric W. and William F. Allman, eds., *Newton at the Bat: The Science in Sports.* New York: Scribner, 1984.

Tenner, Edward, *Why Things Bite Back: Technology and the Revenge of Unintended Consequences.* New York: Alfred A. Knopf, 1996.

Watts, Robert G. and A. Terry Bahill, *Keep Your Eye on the Ball: The Science and Folklore of Baseball.* New York: W. H. Freeman and Co., 1990.

Index

muscle type and, 5
record breaking in, 48, 49
speed variables, 32, 35–36
surface drag and, 35–36,
70
weight and, 4

Table tennis balls, 79, 106
"Talk therapy," 131, 133
Taylor Made golf clubs,
122, 123
Tennis
body type and, 3
collisions in, 52
"King Kong arm," 18
origins of, 100
shoes and, 64
Tennis balls
bounce and, 90–91
court surface and, 92
form drag and, 78
speed of, 79, 107, 112
spinning of, 106
Tennis rackets, 101,
106–114
center of percussion
on, 119
node on, 113
string tension on, 111
sweet spots on, 108–111,
113
vibration in, 109, 113
Titanium golf clubs, 123,
127
Track and field running
fast-twitch muscles and, 6
record breaking in, 48
surface differences,
30–31, 64, 65
technique and, 29
Training
choosing type of, 10
mitochondria increased
by, 9–10
muscle type and, 6
by Olympic athletes,
17–18
for running, 10, 29
See also Overtraining
Trampoline, rotating on

axis on, 44
Transcendent feelings, 137
Transverse (short) axis, 44
"Trash talk," 140
Turbulence, ball speed and,
81, 82–83

Vibration
in baseball bats, 113
center of percussion and,
118–119
in tennis rackets, 109, 113
Violence, among fans,
144–145
Visualization, use of in
sports, 129–130, 131
$VO_{2\ max}$ (maximal oxygen
consumption), 14, 15
Volleyball
body type and, 2
jumping in, 38
knee injuries in, 67

Walking, 16, 27, 28
Water consumption,
exercise and, 17, 25
Weight, 5–6
mass vs., 53–54
type of sport and, 3, 4
Weight gain
aging and, 12, 16
muscle mass and, 12
steroid use and, 21
Weight lifting
aging and, 12
body type and, 2, 3
muscle development
and, 9
muscle type and, 5, 9
Weight training,
by runners, 29
Whackers
balls and, 101–103, 106
baseball bats, 115–122
center of percussion on,
118–119
golf clubs, 122–127
tennis rackets, 101,
106–114
Wimbledon, volley length

at, 91, 92
Women. See Gender
Worth Incorporated,
aluminum bat by, 119
Wrestling, weight and, 4

Yoga, 131

Credits and Acknowledgments

Design by Gary Crounse
Illustrations by David Barker
Production by Stacey Luce
Edited at the Exploratorium by Pat Murphy
Main text by Susan Davis
Sidebars by Sally Stephens (except as noted)
Sidebar on page 138–139 by Charles Carlson
Sidebars on pages 46 and 50–51 by Pearl Tesler
Sidebars on pages 8, 11, 14, 15, 17, 19, 25, 80–81, 91, 93, 96, 97, 104–105 by
Pat Murphy

Image Credits

Page 2: Annie Leibovitz; page 7 (both): courtesy of Terrie Williams; page 12:
courtesy of Pax Beale; pages 24, 52: AP/Wide World Photos; pages 26, 29, 39, 42,
98: Rod Searcey; pages 51, 93, 97, 105: Amy Snyder; pages 58, 76, 88: courtesy
of the San Francisco 49ers; pages 79, 120: courtesy of the San Francisco Giants/
Martha Jane Stanton; page 80 (top), 81 (top): courtesy of Milton Van Dyke; page
80 (bottom): courtesy of the *Journal of the Physical Society of Japan;* page 81 (bottom left and right): courtesy Onera; page 84: courtesy Thomas J. Mueller; page
90: courtesy Mary Jo Sminkey; pages 100, 124: Harold E. Edgerton; page 128:
NBA photo by D. Bernstein; page 135: NBA photo by Nathaniel S. Butler; pages
138, 139: courtesy of Paul Doherty.

Acknowledgments

Susan Davis would like to thank her husband, Peter Brand, for his love and fine
ideas; her family, for their constant support; Phoebe, for her wonderful compan-
ionship; and Pat Murphy for her wacky, but always very insightful, guidance.
Sally Stephens would like to thank her family for their support and acknowledge
her dog, Skates, who assisted in her studies of the motion of different balls
through the air during spirited games of fetch. Both Susan and Sally would like
to thank the following people for sharing their expertise: Carlton Anderson, Jr.,
Anthony Bartowksi, Hal Bateman, Pax Beale, Jane Cappaert, Steve Doberstein,
Dr. William Evans, Clark Gaines, Dr. David Janda, Joe Lamb, George Lundberg,
George Manning, Glenn McMicken, Robert Mitchell, Jeff Moore, Brad Patterson,
Bob Prichard, Jim Ross, Dr. Jeffrey Ross, Dick Rugge, Ron Sauerhoft, Barbra
Schulte, Dr. Stephen Seiler, Bernard Soriano, Dr. Diane Stevens, and Dr. Paul
Williams.

For their assistance with photos and images, above and beyond the call of duty,
we would like to thank Palm Press, Milton Van Dyke, Onera, Mary Jo Sminkey,
Thomas J. Mueller, Rod Searcey, Stanford University Athletics Department, San
Francisco 49ers, San Francisco Giants, NBA Photos, Pax Beale, Terrie Williams,
Paul Doherty, and Annie Leibovitz.

Special thanks to David Sobel at Holt for his editing expertise. Also, thanks to
the many members of the Exploratorium staff who contributed time, ideas, and
expertise to this book. We would particularly like to thank Gary Crounse for his

design expertise and Buddhist calm in times of great stress; Dave Barker for his baseball expertise and skill in translating abstract concepts into entertaining illustrations; Stacey Luce for her daring design rescue at the eleventh hour; Amy Snyder for her photographs; Mark Nichol for his photo research; Megan Bury for her fact-checking and photo research; Charles Carlson and Karen Kalumuck for reviewing the manuscript from the biologist's perspective; Kurt Feichtmeir for his budgeting acumen; Pearl Tesler for her writing assistance; Ruth Brown for her sage advice; Ellen Klages for her careful copyediting; and Ellyn Hament for her valiant attempts to catch every last typo. Finally, thanks to Exploratorium physicists Paul Doherty and Thomas Humphrey for sharing their physics expertise and secret tricks. We couldn't have done it without you!

About the Authors

Susan Davis has written about odd scientific subjects, such as canine sports medicine, the male battle of the bulge, and the secret lives of ants, for *Sports Illustrated, American Health, The Washington Post,* and other publications. A San Franciscan, she runs, and rides both bikes and horses.

Sally Stephens, Ph.D., trained to be a professional astronomer before deciding she'd rather write about science. She plays softball and basketball, swims, water-skis, cheers for the San Francisco 49ers, and reads the sports pages from front to back every day.

About the Exploratorium

The Exploratorium, San Francisco's museum of science, art, and human perception, is a place where people of all ages make discoveries about the world around them. The museum has over 600 exhibits, and all of them run on curiosity. You don't just look at these exhibits—you experiment with them. At the Exploratorium's exhibits, you can play with a captive tornado, generate an electric current, see what's inside a cow's eye, and investigate hundreds of fascinating natural phenomena.

Each year, over half a million people visit the museum. Through programs for teachers, the Exploratorium also encourages students to learn by asking their own questions and experimenting to find the answers. Through publications like this one, the Exploratorium brings the excitement of learning by doing to people everywhere.

Visit the Exploratorium's home page on the World Wide Web at:

www.exploratorium.edu

Next time you are in San Francisco, come visit the Exploratorium!